Travels in the Time of Trump

Paula DiPerna

First published in 2018 by Endeavour Media Ltd.

This edition published in 2019 by Endeavour Media Ltd.

Table of Contents

Dedicated to the open road of open minds

Chapter 1

Not Scranton Lace

The trip started as I rolled north along the Hudson River in New York, the smoking cold water surface the hint of the coming winter I did not want. October was fleeting, but the river is always glorious, a mirror of changing colors and yet a steady reassurance. The wide breadth of the waterway tricked Henry Hudson into thinking it was a passage to the great riches of the East and would lead him through the mysterious landmass in his way, North America as it turned out.

The river proved to be a dead end for the audacious 16th century navigator, who instead laid claim to the wild and verdant island of Manhattan for the Dutch and changed the course of history anyway.

My train creaked and slunk along, a haggard lifeline for commuters. All along the tracks, rusted bits of iron and scrap hung like broken arms along the river banks. I closed my eyes to the ruins. After all, the train was taking me where I was headed and I could swallow once again the evidence that no one seemed to be bringing this railroad into the 21st century.

Travel is what I live for at times: the ebb and flow of leaving home for a purpose, for a point. I have no plants, no pets, no children, and though there have been plenty of cozy lovers, none of them stayed or neither did I, with as many reasons as hours in a day that could be spent trying to analyze why. So now the world is my lover and neither of us can leave.

Yes, I am bound to myself and what is around me and so, even if I try to close my eyes and wish away evil or ugliness that may be coming to pass, my eyes don't close and it can be time to hit the road.

This time, the point of my travel was political—to canvass voters for Hillary Clinton in Scranton, Pennsylvania during the 2016 US Presidential election. Pennsylvania is a treasure trove of 20 electoral votes in the US Electoral College, that odd intermediary body that allots each state in the U. S. electoral votes based on population, a compromise crafted when the Constitution was written so that the President would be elected neither directly by the people—deemed too volatile—nor indirectly by members of the Congress—deemed too distant and potentially partisan. Also, in theory, the Electoral College gives even the smallest states an important national role. The least populous, such as Wyoming or West Virginia, have at least three electoral votes—in that every state has two US Senators and at least one member of the House of Representatives—and the largest, such as California, as many as 55. The winner of the Presidency must garner 270 of the 538 possible electoral votes, in whatever combination of states.

Scranton itself and Pennsylvania overall were once lock-on in Hillary Clinton's favor, solidly and seemingly irrevocably Democratic, the proverbial 'blue state'. But Donald Trump's outsider campaign and Clinton's own mis-steps had reversed her momentum and she needed every vote she could get.

Trump. The word derives from the 16th century French, 'tromper', meaning to trick or deceive, just like the 'trompe d'oeil' where the eye is made to see what is not there, a foreground as a background, or three dimensions of depth when, in fact, there is only one.

A trump is a trick. On the other hand, to trump someone is to get the upper hand; to play the trump card is to win with a dashing flourish. Of course, Donald Trump, the real estate baron, surely preferred the trump card definition but as he campaigned and got closer to the nomination of his party in 2016, trickster seemed more like it. Tromp d'oeil, trump card, trumpet—any use of the word was all right with me except *President* Trump.

Yet, that's what I could envision no matter how much I wanted to believe otherwise.

According to Google, the forebears of the family of Donald Trump were once known as Drumpf in medieval Germany, but Trump's grandfather, Friedrich, simplified the name to Trump when he passed through Ellis Island in 1885 en route to make his fortune in America, just another immigrant with a reason and desire to leave home. That first American Trump had settled in California, running a chain of Gold Rush restaurants complete with private side rooms where prostitutes could tilt with miners, it is said. The former Drumpf begot Donald Trump's father, Fred Trump, a real estate kingpin in Queens, New York, charged in the 1970s with racial redlining to keep non-whites out of his housing developments. And so three generations of Trumps later, I was on the road.

I picked up my car at Garrison, a quaint village about 30 miles north of New York City where I usually park rather than drive it into the New York

City traffic, and headed due west on I-84. It's a straight shot across the state line into Pennsylvania and night fell quickly and silently once it started, like an arrow on the earth.

There were long stretches of road with no other cars at all and the road was deeply pocked with holes and rugged with cracks. Maybe this part of the road is closed, I thought, and I am the only driver who doesn't know? There were hardly any road signs, and the yellow road stripes meant to divide the lanes were long since faded away. My Honda felt like a spaceship in the void—I was squinting half the time through a grimy rain to make out the curve of the road and what might be ahead.

I have yet to buy a GPS and so I wondered if, because so many drivers now depend on GPS to take them where they want to go, maybe the keepers of American roads think there is no longer any reason to refurbish road signs and lane lines to keep us from crashing. That would be cynically consistent with the constant theme of the day that public budgets need to be cut—let the drivers manage on their own.

Even though I should probably have concentrated strictly on my driving, my mind did drift to what I had once heard from a retired four star US Army General, Wesley Clark, who had himself been a candidate for President in 2004. Clark, who had served as Supreme Allied Commander of NATO from 1997 to 2000, had run for the Democratic nomination in a short-lived, misbegotten foray into politics. A highly credible candidate in my view, he somehow got miniaturized the more he campaigned. He had a weak team of political beginners and no habit of soundbite politics, though he also said, when we spoke about it some years later, "by the time I ran, the good people had been taken." Perhaps true, but surely there had been some top-notch campaign strategists still to be found. But it is true that by the time Clark finally decided to toss his hat into the ring that year, there were already nine other candidates in the running, including Senator John Kerry of Massachusetts, Vermont Governor Howard Dean, and civil rights leader Al Sharpton—the last time, in fact, the Democrats had put up such an expansive menu of choices. Still, no doubt Clark would have made a fine President if he had known the political ropes, for he had a sharp ear for the dismay brewing in America even then.

When he was still his own man and not yet an official candidate, Clark gave a wise and impassioned speech during the summer of 2003 in Lake Placid, New York, a tiny tranquil village where loons land on the lake in the evening without the hint of a ripple and then croon on.

9

Here the Democratic Party had convened a Rural Forum that attracted some of the Presidential contenders. Of those who attended, Clark had the most stature, and as he had not yet officially declared his candidacy, he was not subject to the equal time constraints the party had imposed on the formal candidates and so was asked to give the keynote speech to set the stage.

Clark rose eloquently to the occasion, relaxed and loquacious, without a hint of military bluster. He drew upon a cornucopia of anecdotes to make his points, gathered over years of worldly experience that seemed deeply relevant to civilian life. But his closing remark was to me the most haunting harbinger.

He told us of his last day in uniform on his base, the day before he retired from the Army, when he went to the military barber who had been cutting Clark's hair for years. Clip, clip went the story. Clark said that when the haircut was done, the barber looked directly at Clark and said, "General, I wish you the best but I feel a little sorry for you." Clark wondered why. "Because out there," replied the barber, "no one is in charge."

As I crept along on the highway to Scranton, I had that same disquieting sensation. The US seemed to have entered an 'anything goes' mode of leadership, running out of post-World War II vigor and stature, where venerable banks like Wells Fargo could get away with instructing employees to set up fake accounts for customers and then charge those customers real fees, pocketing the money as sales. Accountability? Evaded. Jail time for the executives in charge? None.

'Deferred maintenance' had become the euphemism for avoidance, and not just neglect of the rubbly road beneath my wheels, but civic and social infrastructure too was also crumbling, the institutions that underpin and serve the flow and function of democracy.

Yet, we must be careful what we wish for. The Trump phenomenon derived, I'm sure, from the craving some Americans had for order that would not only take charge, but expunge the forces they believed were eating into their lives and well-being, immigrants being target number one. Still, to crave that someone is in charge can also be a softer craving for simple common sense. To wish that someone is in charge is, in my view, can be simply to wish to be reassured that someone is alert to what we hold in common. That our needs and dreams are not invisible to those with the power to take care.

Out there, had said the military barber, no one is in charge. Headed into Scranton in the rain, I knew the barber was surely right.

Fortunately, soon, I could do without road signs since the hotel jumped out of the dark once I got close. The massive hotel building had once served as the Scranton railroad station, now listed on the National Register of Historic Places, and was visible from miles away like a temple over the city. I parked as close as I could to the entrance, which meant facing a seedy saloon across the street.

The hotel lobby had a Tiffany glass ceiling and walls of gleaming swirling beige-brown marble bordered all around with glazed porcelain murals from the workshop of the legendary early 20th century American ceramics firm, Grueby Faience. The murals depicted local bucolic scenes long gone. Of these exquisite inlays, someone surely had taken good care. The rest of the hotel was threadbare though, by comparison, more notable against the original majestic marble vision. Knowing the Trump-Clinton election here was so close gave me the feeling of being in another country, not just a neighboring state.

My room was adequate but drab, with windows on the parking lot and saloon—hardly reason to kickback and linger. I headed to dinner—a first night in a new place always needs a beginning. I had a thick chicken soup and crisp salad with a glass of Merlot in the lobby restaurant where the waiter could not have been nicer or more relaxed.

The next morning I headed off to Clinton headquarters—207 North Washington Street. It was easy walking distance but I made a right instead of a left and found myself floundering around various neighborhoods. I decided I could spare some time to make something useful out of the mistake and wandered about a bit.

There had been only five houses in the town in 1840 when the Scranton brothers began investing here, but the city that would eventually bear their name was situated in the middle of a mother lode of anthracite coal. This natural treasure trove kicked off much American heartland industry, including steel and railroads and all prosperity that followed in the region until the crash of American manufacturing in the late 1980s. Scranton was a prototype blue-collar town, Vice-President Joe Biden, who had been born there, had trumpeted when he had been campaigning in Scranton with Hillary Clinton that summer.

But just as blue collar manufacturing bled from the US so economic life had bled from Scranton. The idea of living wages had also gone out the window, along with the constant erosion of the idea of unions. "Unions stand in the way of business" ... "unions make it too expensive to hire American workers" ... "union demands mean we have to move factories abroad" became regular refrains in the era of President Ronald Reagan, who had famously dealt a blow to American unions by firing 11,000 air traffic controllers who had gone on strike in 1981, leading to the decertification of the Controllers Union itself. By the time Donald Trump was a candidate, only roughly 10% of US workers belonged to unions. It is true that labor unions have been corrupt and heavy-handed and are no certain answer to worker concerns, but minus unions, workers have little organized voice on their behalf and have to settle only for the wages and benefits employers are willing to pass along. Minus unions, workers are beggars.

To play to this sense of powerless among worried workers in the coal industry around the country, including Pennsylvania, Trump had been blaming the demise of the coal economy on climate change legislation that restricted the burning of fossil fuels. Trump had been campaigning that he would "bring back those coal jobs" in a disingenuous message mish-mash that ignored the truth that coal had been displaced as an energy source more by cheap natural gas than environmental regulations. Not to mention that coal mining is a most dangerous occupation and burning coal is smutty, gritty and, ideally, to be avoided whenever possible.

Also, Ronald Reagan had so effectively cast government regulation as the chief obstacle to economic prosperity, most Republicans had run on that basic premise for the last two decades. It was easy for Trump to climb on their shoulders, arguing for further dismantling of government agencies and firing up his followers with his sneering promise to "drain the swamp".

But would these bromides play in Pennsylvania, a battleground state that had not gone Republican in a Presidential election since 1988?

Downtown Scranton had plenty of gracious rambling houses and streets lined with trees that lent shade just where it needed to be. There was not much of the bustle I love about cities, but my errant stroll gave me the sense that all could be right with the world.

Finally, I gave in to purpose and headed to the right street. But, I could not spot the campaign office. Finally, hardly calling attention, there it was: a tiny sign just about whispering 'Clinton/President'.

Inside, also no buzz. None of the usual campaign hub-bub. Instead, a dozen youngish men and women were typing madly on their laptops as if writing code or playing the horses. No one looked up.

One woman with triple silvery ear cuffs on her earlobe that faced me stopped typing and looked up to say hello. I was expected, so she called on her mobile to the back room to tell the volunteer coordinator I had arrived.

I looked around for buttons, posters, stickers, the usual paraphernalia— almost no campaign stuff. "We're waiting for more," the woman told me and turned back to her computer.

Canvassing voters is the art of counting and the goal is to make sure that any and every voter who can vote and would vote for your candidate does vote. Canvassing is part of the turnout machine and the canvasser's job is to make sure that any legal, living, breathing voter actually goes to cast a ballot. This means the canvasser must go house to house to pinpoint votes. Canvassing is politics at its retail starting point.

The work can be lonely and demanding, and canvassers generally are assigned to work in pairs. Like diving or swimming alone, canvassing alone can be hazardous if you get into trouble.

I had canvassed voters once before, for Senator John Kerry in Columbus, Ohio—still an all-important swing state—after Kerry won the 2004 Democratic nomination and ran against incumbent President George W. Bush. Kerry had served in the US Senate for three terms, after first coming to public attention in the 1970s as a decorated Vietnam War hero who had nevertheless started the group Vietnam Veterans Against the War. Kerry had served in the US Navy, winning the Purple Heart and other high military honors but came back from his service deeply disillusioned about US intentions in Vietnam, and threw his experience and renown into anti-war activities. In a heart-rending testimony before the US Congress, the young John Kerry had challenged: "How do you ask a man to be the last man to die for a mistake?" There was no good answer.

In Columbus, I had been teamed up with a volunteer who had traveled roughly 2000 miles from Slave Lake in Alberta, Canada to lend a hand. She was an American citizen who had so rejected the Vietnam War, she had left the US. entirely to make a new life in Canada, eventually marrying and settling down to run a hunting and fishing lodge.

We trudged from house to house, and one afternoon as we took an apple break—I had brought a stash of luscious Gala apples from upstate New York—she told me that she had come to canvass for Kerry because "I felt I owed him something." She went on to say, "He served our country, for me, then came home and tried to end the war, for me. This was the least I could do to pay him back."

In the end, John Kerry lost Ohio, a perennial critical swing state, and thus the US. Presidency, by a mere 120,000 votes, not many more people than the average attendance at an Ohio State University football game.

I still have the notebook where I had done the electoral math in the vain hope that Kerry could offset the loss of Ohio if he won the electoral votes of New Mexico and Colorado and other smaller western states. He didn't.

But for the Clinton-Trump contest, I did not feel like canvassing with a stranger. This time, the prospect that Trump could win seemed even worse than the prospect of a Bush re-election. I thought I'd rather be with a reliable soulmate and so I let my friends know my plans. One friend, and my personal physician to boot, T'nette, decided to come along. She too had the Hillary-may-lose jitters and she also already knew Scranton a bit since her husband's parents had lived there. Plus, she loved the railroad station hotel.

T'nette drove to Scranton separately and we met up, canvassing by day and catching up on girl talk by night. Both of us had the need to feel useful, and she also brought her clinician's focus to the task at hand.

And despite the joke often made that candidates should find a way to get the dead to vote, canvassing is dead serious. Voters have to be legally registered, for one thing, and that's a right and a privilege not to be joked about. In most countries, citizens are issued a national identity card that makes it infinitely easier to track who is who and also who is not registered. But in the US we have no such identity cards because of our belief that government should not track its citizens formally or universally. We are tracked when we file Federal taxes or collect Federal benefits, or other Federal interactions. Otherwise, most Americans are invisible to the controls of our Federal system even though, of course, in the digital age of intricate sharing of data bases, anonymity is almost non-existent de facto. But, so far, other than the national Census every ten years, it is still not our Federal government's policy to keep an official roll call of its people. Voter registration for all elections is managed by the states.

So repeatedly I was told by the Clinton campaign staff that when I spoke to voters, I had to remind them to bring some form of official identification to the voting place, such as a driving license, employment letter or an electric bill to corroborate their legal address. A key bit of counsel. This was to make sure our Hillary voters were fortified with proof of identity in case the validity of their registration was challenged, and talk of possible pro-Trump electoral mischief was definitely in the air even though, at that time, the story that the government of Russia might be hacking into the election had yet to break.

I got clear on the instructions, but didn't hit the streets until T'nette arrived.

We were given explicit direction on how to do our job. First of all, verify that the voter listed on our registered Democratic voter sheets actually exists and is inclined to vote for HRC. Speak only to that person and if that person is not home or does not come to the door, return later. Don't leave messages and don't speak to wives on behalf of husbands or husbands on behalf of wives or partners on behalf of partners, no messages at all—"lots of men never tell their wives and the wife is usually the registered Democrat," we were advised. And be sure the voters know their polling place location and find out if they need help getting there. Especially, keep track of who might need a ride.

The workers at the campaign office definitely knew the basics of canvassing, but still, the silence of the headquarters gave me the creeps. I felt no election passion, no pro-Hillary juice and none of the zest I had expected having heard so much about the strength of Hillary's canny ground operation. Headquarters felt more like a statistics lab than a go-for-the-jugular political hub.

That flatness, as it turned out, was a bad omen.

We set out, however, obedient good worker bees, armed with a clipboard and precinct maps fresh from the copy machine, each letter size. But there was no giant battle plan map with all precincts in Scranton on the wall at the office to show us where in the city we were headed or where we fit; no big picture, so we had the sense of working the toenail of an elephant.

We used T'nette's car because she did have a GPS and our one-page maps were hopeless in giving us a sense of where to get started.

"Go two miles and turn …" intoned the metallic GPS advisor. Lucky for us—that's how we found our way.

But our Scranton was not at all the Scranton of downtown and tall reassuring shade trees I had stumbled around on day one. Our precincts were home to voters who lived far down the social totem pole.

Above all else, canvassing depends on ringing doorbells, but that was our first sign of trouble and a master message on what blue collar America had become. Hillary's campaign was counting on us ringing doorbells but there were almost no doorbells to ring.

At house after house, the bells hung pathetically limp, torn out of the wall. Many others were still in place but not working. We pressed and pressed, hearing nothing and surely not that familiar ding-dong chime or buzz we should have heard, even if no one was home. More dead silence to worry about.

We were assigned streets of mainly modest one- and two-family houses, no massive apartment blocks or public housing of the rundown type that is known around the US as 'the projects'.

But our first street was blighted enough. Once pretty houses were ratty and in need of paint. Boxes of trash and what appeared to be donated shoes were piled on a porch otherwise nicely kept. But so many porches were unswept, with strips of outdoor rug coming untacked or entirely ripped up and rolled out of the way in moldy tatters. Beer cans littered the grass; bottle caps littered the steps. Empty plastic milk bottles lay here and there, as if tossed in by a hurricane. Many neighborhoods felt like way stations where only squatters came and went. Compared to our hotel only a few miles away, we had entered a zone of disenfranchisement where work did not seem to pay off in being able to keep up your house. The decline seemed broad and extensive.

I had begun reading the journalist George Packer's excellent article in the New Yorker magazine on how the Clinton-Trump Presidential race had become such a close call. He analyzed the socio-economics, writing:

'"Working class" ... has become a euphemism. It once suggested productivity and sturdiness. Now it means downwardly mobile, poor, even pathological. A significant part of the W.W.C. [White Working Class] has succumbed to the ills that used to be associated with the black urban 'underclass': intergenerational poverty, welfare, debt, bankruptcy, out-of-wedlock births, trash entertainment, addiction, jail, social distrust, political cynicism, bad health, unhappiness, early death. The heartland towns that abandoned the Democrats in the Eighties to bask in Ronald Reagans morning sunlight; the communities that Sarah Palin, on a 2008 campaign stop in Greensboro, North Carolina, called 'the best of America ... the real America'—those places were hollowing out, and politicians didn't seem to notice. A great inversion occurred.'

Here in Scranton, he was as if looking over my shoulder.

The city was trying hard, a typical urban heart that had had its industrial aorta ripped out and was trying to rebuild its health with upscale fusion food restaurants and IT incubators. Coal mining and manufacturing had once generated enough economic growth to warrant grand downtown buildings, now vestiges in the skyline, like the *Scranton Times*, whose modernistic tower ushered in the era or radio and TV and the city's first skyscraper, the Electric Building, with its giant 'Scranton: The Electric City' neon billboard still shining at night for miles.

We tried to take joy in the Christmas wreaths on some of the doors, at least a sign the people who lived there were alert to the season and good cheer, except when I saw a plastic wreath hung by a bent wire coat hanger, I lost the Christmassy bounce in my step. It occurred to me that maybe these wreaths were not hung early at all, but instead forgotten remnants from the year before.

That was more likely since it was not even yet Halloween.

We did the best we could without doorbells, and threw ourselves into the task, feeling new respect for census-takers and thankful for the basics of rainproof knapsacks and sensible shoes.

One of our routes took us near Eddie's Garage and Diner, where Eddie and a friend took in all kinds of engines and cars for repair and served breakfast too. Eddie's announced itself with two tall plastic palm trees posted on either side of the shop like Corinthian columns and someone, maybe Eddie himself, hosed down the sidewalk vigorously, dislodging every scrap of stray paint and tar.

Our canvass address was a few doors down from Eddie's, and before we could ring the first bell, our first voter was on her way out, an African American woman with her arms full. She told us how tired she was before we could say a word. She was doing her best to hold onto a red woven plastic basket, her arms slipping off and the basket nearly tipping away. "See all this laundry?" she asked. "I have a lot because I can't stand to keep dirty clothes in my house. Dirty dishes either."

She was headed out again even though she had just gotten back from shopping, and she told us she had bought a giant size box of dog food 'crunch' for her neighbor's dog—they had three dogs between them.

I guessed that where doorbells have been de-wired, or pulled out, people had watchdogs instead. She knew exactly where to go to vote and recited the address back to us perfectly. But a ride, oh yes, that would be a big help because, as she said, "I do want to get there so I can make my vote count."

I noted her name and address preciously.

We went out canvassing even on Sunday morning, hoping more voters would be home. It being Halloween, it seemed as if democracy itself might be in costume, dressed in ghost wrap deteriorating in the wind that sent dust and debris across the porches where nobody was home and where maybe nobody lived anymore.

Some homes were decorated full bore, their trappings a commentary on life by the people who lived there, I had to assume. There were some classic orange and black scary goblins, but way too many guns and skull and crossbones for my taste, even whole porches draped in military camouflage. Halloween had turned our parts of Scranton weird and threatening, and I fantasized our nation as sideshow, complete with bearded ladies and inflatable people with hot purple tongue studs, and 100% tattooed chests, their outsized muscles rippling under shredding tee shirts.

We were not in the pretty parts of town, for sure, and we weren't turning up much pay dirt in terms of Clinton voters either, although T'nette, a devoted gardener, tried to keep up her optimism. When she spotted a well-kept lawn or flower garden, she tended to say as we hopped up the stairs, "This one should be good for us."

But there were poignant touches too. We stepped up onto one porch to find a Latino man absently watching his 11-year-old daughter scribbling in her coloring book as she sucked on a lollipop that left her tongue the fuzzy pastel mix of an Impressionistic sky. He knew where to vote but said he had not yet made up his mind.

On that street, one tidy house had a large lump of coal as a centerpiece on the lawn.

It was obvious how these once white working class neighborhoods had changed. Scranton had originally been settled mostly by white Europeans—Italians, Lithuanians, Russians and Poles—and if an established family was not comfortable with Scranton's changing demographics, home streets might well feel alien.

In an area with quite a few Slavic names on our sheet, a Catholic Church had become a Shiva Center, not far from the Shiva convenience store. Still new arrivals meant new energy, and the Mansour market, on the corner of the same street, was an oasis of good coffee and good repair. We had a quick lunch there, and met a special education teacher, a white woman who was waitressing because her nine-year-old son was chronically ill and needed intensive medical care and she needed to make more money to cover the bills. "He takes all my attention," she confessed, "but I love him so."

One day we began canvassing on the wrong street but didn't notice the error for a while because the names on the houses matched our canvas sheets—Patels. Patel porches with Patel swings. In Scranton you could be canvassing the wrong houses and wrong streets and still be canvassing Patels.

The work required lots of walking, not to mention driving and trying to park, getting in and out of the car, lost then found. It was hardly grueling but inflicted its own form of burnout. We retreated to our hotel to digest the experience of the day. But it was not all that easy to disconnect.

Almost everywhere I had the sense of people pushing against the odds. Back in the hotel, I watched a harried hard-working woman who was too overweight for her clothes slugging away making coffee alone at the busy hotel coffee bar, trying to keep track of all the variations on flavored latte shots.

"Ok. Mocha caramel. Salted or not?" she asked a customer wistfully.

Meanwhile, as she dutifully added all the trimmings that made the coffee that looked more like an ice cream sundae, other guests were clamoring for service right then. She held them off courteously but it took her three minutes to figure out how to get her digital cash register to ring up an item that cost $2.12.

The obesity epidemic in America was clearly evident too.

The hotel was a popular wedding venue, and one day I had to use the piano in the lobby as a desk to make a quick note since all the sitting nooks were taken. In one sofa corner, two men, each Buddha-sized, sat, one empty-handed, the other holding a super-sized latte cup loaded with cream as they chatted amiably to each other. And in the matrimonial dining room off the lobby, the chairs were set already pulled out from under the table, as if ready to accommodate the overweight guests who would come in soon for supper.

But the next morning the white satin wedding trappings were stowed away and the wedding guests checked out en masse.

We headed out for another day.

We had already had one encounter with a husband who we doubted would tell his wife we had been there. A burly white man had come to the door when we knocked—we had pretty much given up on the doorbells.

Gruffly, he told us "she's not here" when we asked for the woman whose name was on our sheet. When we followed our guidelines and asked to know when she might be home, he just said "she doesn't want to talk to you", and slammed the door.

So, we were a bit more ready the next time, but if you learn nothing else from canvassing it's that every house and family is different, every story its own.

Next time a man came to the door we were prepared, we thought.

"May we speak to Mrs …?"

"She's ill and can't come to the door." But he kept the door open.

We pressed.

"Are you taking care of her?" we asked intrusively.

"Yes."

"And will you help her get to the polls."

"Yes."

"And may we ask if you plan to vote."

"Of course."

"And may we ask for whom?"

Now we were violating every rule, and it set off an edifying torrent. It turned out that the man, white, was a World War II veteran who told us he had worked in cryptography. He talked about how tough the war had been, how sad to see so many people killed. About the election he said he was undecided still. Though leaning toward Hillary Clinton he was bothered by the fact that she had used a private email server as Secretary of State and the possibility that government secrets had been violated.

"I would have been sent to Leavenworth riding on the back of a dump truck," he told us, visualizing himself in military prison, "if I so much as let out a call sign."

"It's up to Comey now, I guess," he added, referring to the then head of the US Federal Bureau of Investigation, who was leading an investigation into the Clinton email debacle.

"I see you are paying attention," quipped my doctor pal.

"Don't you think I should?" said he.

We were humbled. Here was a retired vet taking care of an ailing wife maybe more sick than he knew, following political events so closely we had little to offer.

At times we got so frustrated with no answers at the doors even on the weekend that we resorted to trying the neighbors. But that backfired often—at one house, a white woman shooed us away from trying to get an answer next door. She came out in her pajamas to chase us, one pants leg longer than the other dragging along the grass.

We kept at it, but still came across very few people on our list.

Very often when women opened the door it was only to say "he doesn't live here anymore"—about a son, or brother or husband or boyfriend, gone or just not wanting to show himself to strangers.

And then the worst of our experiences, I'd say, one day when we persisted with a bell that actually did ring because we heard some responsive sounds that seemed to be getting closer and closer. We waited eagerly. Then, an elderly white woman opened the door, her wrists the size of dumbbells. She seemed to have some kind of fierce edema and she could barely move. She had struggled to the door and was so disappointed to find it was us rather than someone or something that could help her. T'nette did give her some basic general medical advice and we slunk away. We were disgusted with ourselves.

We met our one and only newly minted 18-year-old voter, who proudly told us he was about to vote for the first time for President. Fighting cynicism, "Anyone but Trump" said he. He added he was inclined toward the spoiler Libertarian Party candidate Gary Johnson. That he was attracted to the Libertarians was dismaying enough to me in itself, but what we said was that a vote for a third party would be the same as throwing his vote away.

"I'll do my research," he says, "I know it's always the lesser of two evils … I'm kind of sorry my first election is like this." So were we.

It was no more satisfying working the phone banks. Call after call, no answer. Call after call, voicemail. Call after call, no way to check whether a number was accurate because no way to check cell phone numbers. And when someone did actually answer, on call after call, many said they weren't voting or were not registered. I had to hope that the campaign was doing better with its social media outreach. A few hours of calling yielded one or two "yes, a ride would be nice" replies, a few live voters for a few hours of work.

It seemed we were getting nowhere, even though the campaign staff exuded feel-good gratitude and reassured us that every hour we had spent on the streets of Scranton had helped. Once T'nette left, I had not much further zeal for canvassing.

I decided to devote my last Scranton days to an exploit of a wholly different kind. It is a long way from canvassing coal town to lace, but I had become fascinated by the saga of Scranton Lace, founded in 1890, and once a thriving Scranton textile company and the nation's leading producer of Nottingham-manufactured lace. Scranton Lace employed 1400 people in its heyday and was so prosperous its factory complex had its own theater, bowling alley and gym for the employees. And, in a fitting link that took my Scranton journey full circle, Hillary Clinton's father, Hugh Rodham, had once worked as a manager in the now defunct lace company. But that had not been my Scranton Lace impetus.

I had learned about Scranton Lace long before, by accident, when I had been browsing in a photo gallery in Massachusetts that specializes in vintage photographs in search of a wedding present for a young man I knew. I was soon mesmerized by the black-and-white photos of exquisite lace tablecloths with delicate patterns of sheaves of wheat billowing or tropical palm fronds bending, all in fine detail, pure white ineffably fine lace shot against pure black background.

Eugene Greenfield, the gallery owner and photo expert, explained that these were photos of Scranton Lace samples. The company had commissioned the shots for sales purposes from photographers of the day, and the photographers used their lace photography work to better understand the technical parameters of rapidly advancing photo lens technology—what detail could a given lens capture without blurring, what setting, shutter speed, and so forth. When photography was a manual process, each photograph was an experiment and the exquisite intricacy of lace gave a camera a demanding test.

Greenfield had numerous boxes of photos of Scranton Lace samples—he had bought them at an auction to save them from oblivion.

The company, however, did hit an oblivion in 2002 even more permanent than the coal industry and Scranton Lace is no more, its jobs and lacy delights all gone.

The corporate archives, though, Greenfield had told me, were in a town called Waverly, just outside of Scranton, and I decided to head out there to rinse my head of broken doorbells.

Waverly was everything our canvassing precincts were not—paint still on the clapboards, no bottle caps on the steps. Property values looked high and steady, and where our precincts had had very few Hillary signs, in

Waverly there were plenty of Trump signs. Pennsylvania was going Republican red right here before my eyes.

I settled into my lace research and felt that surge of satisfaction that goes with a new-found passion. I found more samples showing bouquets and leaves and also bold graphic designs with a contemporary feel. Sheer, dazzling, delicate beauty sprung from human imagination. I was so glad to be reminded of it. I spent half a day with those bits of lace, and left full of joy as if the election were not still a looming worry.

Then, thud, back to earth. A Trump banner at least fifty feet long had been pulled taut along the highway service road, a troubling backdrop to a huge decommissioned military tank displayed along the highway—Trump and tanks, lace and artillery.

I retraced my drive back to New York on I-84, this time in sunny daylight. Images returned: so much junk on porches, deflated ghost balloons, unpacked packaging, air going out of the tires of America and me eating Greek yoghurt with honey nevertheless in a hotel not far away. Each doorbell disconnected took me back to the shortcomings of leadership and the pride of nation that seemed to be slipping away.

All in all, what did we accomplish with our canvassing? The few Hillary supporters we met were determined. The rest … who knew, but seemingly living mostly at the margins of life where voting might not be a priority on Election Day; struggling people left to their own devices.

And on election night, the outcome was all too clear too soon.

Friends and I had assembled at T'nette's to watch the returns, hoping to have a Trump defeat to celebrate even if half our group had never been all that warm to Hillary.

Our potluck supper overflowed with hefty home-cooked heartiness, plenty of warm comfort food, but our mood never rose. Somehow, the premonition had the better of us.

TV commentators kept chalking up electoral results that worsened with every swipe. The pixels were not adding up our way—oh, if only the commentator's fingertips could have conjured up more Hillary Clinton votes. We jumped from pro-Trump Fox TV to CNN to NBC, even to Al Jazeera for a while. One state after the other that should have gone blue went red. Why, oh, why Ohio, indeed. No one dared make a move to uncork the champagne.

Pennsylvania went for Trump. The election was called.

Had our voters gotten there, had anything we had done in Scranton made any difference?

If any, not enough. As I headed home that night, my heart felt broken. I did not even yet know my home county too had gone against Clinton.

The time of Trump was upon us, and I knew nothing would be as I thought it should, for as far and as long as the eye could see. But, where now, did I fit?

Chapter 2

Let the Tanks Guard Louis Vuitton

A love of politics is like any love—to be strong it must be rooted well and yet it must move along and grow with the times. The roots of my love of politics were firm, tracing back to my mother and her own political zest. I'm sure that the election of Donald Trump to the highest office of the land would have nauseated her—she had died long before.

The youngest daughter of an Italian immigrant family, born in the US and committed fiercely to assimilation, my mother threw herself into all the protocols of American democracy, taking any occasion to praise America and all it had to offer if only one would take advantage. She was a diehard Republican and had volunteered every year to help at our Board of Elections whether the election was local or national. Her job was to keep an eye on the polling process, making sure all voters who had questions got accurate answers. She put in a full day, and was always proud to tell me how many voters had been there to cast their ballot. Election Day was holy in our house and off my mother went.

By far, though, the key indelible event was the day I saw my mother literally skipping down the long hallway of our apartment, like a young girl just given a ruby red rose. In her hand was an envelope from the Republican National Committee.

Inside the envelope had been proof positive for my mother that America's systems worked, and if not that anyone could be President, surely that anyone could write to the President.

Which my mother had done. She had rolled a sheet of paper right into her trusty Royal typewriter before my eyes one day, clicking and clacking a letter to the then President, Dwight D. Eisenhower, known as Ike, who was then just getting ready for his re-election campaign. My mother had seen what was about to become an iconic photo of the scruffy sole of the shoe of Adlai Stevenson, the Democratic opponent of Eisenhower, with a big hole in it. The photo had been snapped when Stevenson had crossed his legs, and his campaign had begun to use the photo to suggest that despite his patrician and intellectual bearing, Stevenson walked around with holes in his shoes just like Everyman, maybe even because he, too, could not afford to see the shoemaker to get them fixed. But my mother, who had gifts of quick retort, read that photo another way: To the President, she wrote:

'So ... The Democrats have nominated Adlai E. Stevenson for their Presidential candidate! Now the Republicans have more chance than ever of winning.

Since it appears you are planning to run for re-election, I thought you might be interested in an idea regarding Mr. Stevenson's so-called symbol. I understand that he and his followers are proud to display a shoe, with a hole in the sole. Very funny ... to some. To the average hard-working American citizen a shoe with a hole in the sole is not funny. It indicates poverty and depression and all the terrible demoralizing factors that follow it.

If that is the best Stevenson can offer the American people for the future—a shoe with a hole in it—then 1930 and 1931 will seem like prosperity compared to it.

If a man can't keep his own shoes in repair, how can he expect to keep the state of the Nation in good repair and keep it from getting a 'hole' in its 'soul'? I hope you can use this idea in your campaign, as I am sure there are more Americans who feel as I do about Stevenson's so-called humor.'

Off the letter went addressed simply The President, The White House. Within six weeks, she had received a reply from Sherman Adams, Ike's Chief of Staff, reporting that: *'The President wants me to thank you for your letter. He is grateful for your active interest in his re-election. I am passing on your very interesting suggestion to the Republican National Committee which will, I know, give it careful consideration ...'*

Then, even fewer weeks later, that envelope and her skip down the hall. The Committee had apparently also liked my mother's idea, wasting no time to use it. They sent her a batch of campaign bumper stickers, envelope seals and buttons, all using my mother's theme and expressed as "Think! Don't let this happen to you" circling the hole in Adlai's shoe.

My mother received no payment, or public acknowledgement, not even an invitation to an Ike victory party, but she felt compensated enough by the fact that her suggestion would help re-elect the President, and now she held proof in her hands.

Her joy that day and pride in America was contagious and sent me on my way to political passion too. My mother had remained a Republican throughout her life until the first Bill Clinton race in 1992, when she quietly confessed to me she had crossed party lines to vote Democratic, mostly because she liked Hillary and "that Bill Clinton makes sense."

As for me, though I admire Eisenhower in retrospect, I have never voted Republican for any office and the parade of ill-prepared bombastic candidates in the 2016 Republican primary, all trying to out-Trump Trump made me sick.

Not to mention that I myself had run for the US Congress as a Democrat in 1992—perhaps another reason my mother switched parties that year—in upstate central New York where I have a home and have been locally politically active.

It had also been the Year of the Women, a major effort to elect more women to the US Congress. I felt I could handle the job since at the time I had experience in international affairs, especially environmental policies, giving me quite a bit of interaction with the Congress and Heads of State worldwide. And I felt I could at least do as good a job as the incumbent, who had a lackluster record that did not warrant a free pass. I was the only Democrat running, but my Congressional race grew into a five-way contest, including a far-right candidate who, I felt, would drain votes from the Republican. Just enough of a wild card situation. Carpe diem.

I collected enough signatures from registered Democrats to get my name on the ballot, the first step for any candidate, and secured the endorsement of the local and national Democratic Party. My campaign began rolling along, and volunteers began to join. My campaign took me day and night across the gentle contoured hills of New York, to county fairs and dairy farms, college campuses, barbeques, diners and rallies—anywhere voters gathered. It was grass roots politics at its diverse, intoxicating best—including handshakes, if not kisses, with plenty of babies. I spoke to countless voters, many of whom were self-employed, hardworking people who knew that they needed reliable government despite their suspicion of regulations. And, at the time, in this rural independently minded area, the idea of a single-payer healthcare system, such as the National Health Service in the UK or other similar systems in Europe, long anathema in the United States, then was meeting genuine interest and support. All over the district, voters were frightened about rising healthcare costs and the fragility of their hold on private health insurance.

I also focused on the need to tame the Federal deficit, which had been swollen due to tax cuts for the wealthy and excess defense spending; update antiquated Federal laws that caused dairy farmers to have to sell their products below cost; rework revenue-sharing formulas between the Federal government and local governments that burdened tight local budgets; generate jobs creation through environmental investment; invest in affordable housing and guarantee women's rights. One major local media outlet endorsed me, and others said I was a credible candidate. The campaign was exhausting but exhilarating—as I told voters, "I love life, I have hope and I think we could be doing so much better."

But in the end I could not overcome the incumbent's advantage, though I did win 61,835 votes to his 139,774, in just an eight-week campaign spending only $30K raised from supporters.

Losing was disappointing, but not unexpected, and politics has its humor. I had once asked a local leading Democratic Party supporter why he had not run for office, since he had such a high profile, and he quipped, "I always knew there were plenty of people around who didn't like me, but I never wanted an exact count."

Half full or half empty, the glass of my campaign was all the more reason I found the election of Trump so demeaning. In my experience, most white voters teetering on the economic edge were reasonable and not vitriolic, just yearning for leadership and recognition.

Trump shamelessly whipped them up, though, and fed their frustrations this time and a sense of disenfranchisement among working class white men was the key to his rise. Still, that Trump himself had actually won the Presidency despite his vulgarity and lack of experience and competence hung on me like a yoke. I kept thinking of the climactic scene of Steven Spielberg's film masterpiece, *Schindler's List*, when Schindler, an affluent German who had risked his life and fortune to save 1100 Jews who worked for him from the Nazis, broke down in tears crying, "I could have done more."

I entered the weeks after Election night consumed by remorse, guilt and despair. I did not want to turn to the next page in the book. I felt impotent and deadened.

But I had to get on with my life. I was due to attend yet another global climate change conference, this one in Marrakech, Morocco.

It was dubbed COP-22, meaning the 22nd Conference of the Parties of the Framework Convention on Climate Change, which had been agreed by most of the nations of the world in 1992, and then taken a few years to ratify.

When the Convention had been agreed, I'd been working for oceans pioneer and explorer, Jacques-Yves Cousteau as a writer and his chief policy advisor. We had been deeply involved in securing the adoption of the Convention at Rio, working with the Head of the Conference, the President of Brazil, and pressing President George H. W. Bush, to attend the Rio Summit. In fact, we had two meetings with Bush in the Oval Office, over tea.

Since then, in various roles, I have never been far from the climate change issue, and other environmental issues, trying to advance the ball and tie environmental facts to their sociological and economic context. For one cannot love the earth, I feel, without also loving its people, even when we falter and even though human activities are the inescapable cause of environmental degradation. There are no easy answers to environmental dilemmas now that there are so many people on the planet, and after so many years of ignoring science and postponing remedy. In the developed world, we put off much environmental consideration in favor of blaring build-up of industry, driving today's problems such as climate change and water shortages that threaten to overwhelm all countries, but most especially the poorer countries least equipped to cope.

For all its faults, the United Nations process has remained the sole enterprise that tries to balance out these inequities, providing a forum where richer countries could be reminded regularly about their obligations to the poorer ones.

Of course, UN conferences are often deadly dull, with hours and days spent negotiating wording of single paragraphs in long duplicative international agreements. I often feel that the main function of the UN is to extinguish passions, which is perhaps why it has been able to maintain a rocky global peace, since anyone entering a UN setting full of fire is likely to have that fire hosed down by the tedious monotone of the UN negotiating process.

Still, I've remained committed to the UN cycle on climate change and that has meant attending many COPs, their locations rotating year to year around the world, like an Olympics of global diplomacy.

Morocco had long been established as the venue for COP-22, the first COP after Trump's election.

I had been to Marrakech already once some years ago when tourists were expected to take pleasure in touring leather factories despite the awful spectacle of young boys coated in red and orange dye as they tended blobby hot vats used to color the countless wallets, hassocks and folding coin purses made in Morocco. I had been tagging along then with a friend who had a singing gig in Casablanca. What days of innocence.

The COP trip would be my first foray out of the country since Trump's election—even my luggage felt heavier. I simplify, codify, do not yet Spotify, but I was crossing the ocean to indulge, complain, critique, speak, study and think.

I had gotten up at 4 a.m. in my apartment in New York City to get to the airport to take the day flight to London before heading to Marrakech the next day. I have long since given up short night flights or long non-stop ones. If there is no reason to rush or lose sleep, why do it?

I watched the news and combed the papers in the lounge at JFK airport, which felt the same as always, unchanged by the election so far—coffee available 100 ways, milk too, plenty of whipped cream to pour on the cakes. It felt like an upscale version of the Scranton hotel lobby coffee bar.

But I was aching with worry and no place to put it. I knew it was possible that with the election of Trump, for a while, the US had lost everything.

At least the New York Times had a front page story about cuckoo birds that had been tracked flying from China to Africa when scientists had thought that much distance was for them impossible. Good for the cuckoo birds. Political upsets cannot be our only surprise.

Me, the know-it-all, I wished that Hillary Clinton would lick her wounds and tomorrow announce she was running for Mayor of New York City. But then, I always felt Bill Clinton should have done that too. Neither of them would have had to campaign even for a single day. Their announcement alone would have elected them and being Mayor of New York City is probably America's next best political job after the White House. But that was again more fantasy. The election was only a few days old. Hillary was in retreat.

I felt we were facing a chaotic world, dominated by anger, violence, vitriol and incompetence. One could only hope that Trump himself, a sociopath in some ways but merely a lazy indifferent fat cat in other ways, might soon become fearful that his own revolution could go too far, and that he would restore some semblance of respect for the institutions he so denigrated in his campaign to avoid full-fledged social revolt.

This wish was not about liberalism or conservatism, but about the need to govern from the middle, for only the middle can hold common sense together, and thus the common good. Radical views on either side serve the important purpose of pulling the middle forward, but when one or the other sides wins out, someone like Trump, or worse, is elevated.

Not to mention that Trump lost the popular vote in the US and, in theory, should feel some sense of obligation to the views of voters nationwide who did not vote in his favor. Freedom is so fragile, and only idiots or tyrants play with it, as was compounding around the world as Trump's era began—the nightmare of Duarte in the Philippines, proud and defiant about the fact that he had ordered extra-legal executions of accused criminals, claiming they were drug-dealers or terrorists but scooping his political opponents into the shooting net as well; or Nicholas Maduro in Venezuela, who seemed to get high on the deprivations of his people.

And for many of us who call the USA our home, Trump's election felt like a moment of deep soul-searching. How to spend these four years? More ceaseless opinion-making? More noise? More critique? What?

My flight to London was over in six hours and in a flash I was through the efficient Heathrow immigration and on the Heathrow Express, seamless modern infrastructure conceived with the passenger's convenience in mind. Here, someone definitely had been in charge. The train clerk sold me a ticket at the gate and called me "darling".

I spent the night in Soho, at one of my favorite cozy hotels, where no one was other than freaked out about Trump. "Maybe you will have to come and live right here," said the familiar night clerk as he checked me in. That night was as short on sleep as the night before as I again had a crack-of-dawn flight.

I was back to the airport in another zip train ride the next morning and back into the airport cookie cutter. Ads seem to have taken over any available space in airports, thanks to so-called public-private partnerships, which bring in money to expand airports on the one hand, but at the price of turning over all walls, walkways, gateways and passageways to the service of selling products. But as loudly as the ads scream for attention, everyone seems fixated on their iPhones, playing games or scrolling one-handed as they walk along and pulling and pushing their rolling bags.

On the plane to Morocco I struck up a conversation with various seatmates, all of whom were headed to the same conference, the first COP for some of them, but for me I had to count.

Moroccan customs had set up a COP fast lane, so I was out of the airport quickly enough to catch the end of sunset, a spectacular pink-red so gorgeous I asked my taxi driver to pull over so I could take a picture. But, as often happens, the camera was too late. Better to remember what I'd seen with my own eyes.

My hotel was fine but not the city's best. That was La Mamounia, a traveler's legend, a few minutes away and I was eager to see it on such a lovely evening. At the enormous chaotic traffic circle, a policeman intervened to help me cross, stopping a Caterpillar bulldozer plus a phalanx of motorbikes so I could pass, but still a speeding four-wheel drive truck narrowly missed me as the driver boldly defied the cop.

La Mamounia is straight out of Arabian Nights: gardens of delight, palms and dates trees and dripping flowers, tiled arches and deeply carved wood; the perfect oasis among oases. At last I felt far away from my own time, safe inside the walls. Yet, in less than two minutes, I bumped into people I knew from home, and a friend from Brazil too, so usual are the usual conference attendees. Plinio, the Brazilian, was as stunned as I was. He gave me a big hug and said, "Oh I feel so sorry for you after the Election."

"Thanks," I said weakly, "but I also feel sorry for you!"

We planned to talk further the next day, but I never caught up with him again.

The next morning I planned my usual conference routine, and started my day. But the bathroom in my room seemed to have been designed by a giant. I could barely reach the towel racks from the shower, and only a pole vaulter could have easily cleared the height of the bath tub.

I slipped around but survived. Television news was all Trump, all the time, mounting speculation on his appointees. I flipped it off, then back on again. Trump had indeed announced he had named as his chief counselor and strategic advisor Steven Bannon, founder of the far right nearly fascist website Breitbart News that pumped out conspiracy theories and racist, anti-Semitic diatribes, including that conservative media analyst Bill Kristol was a "renegade Jew". Plus Trump had announced that he'd planned to deport only a mere three million immigrants first chance he got, rather than all the eleven million estimated undocumented immigrants, as he had once promised on the campaign trail. As for women, he vowed again to appoint a Supreme Court justice who would overturn the Roe v. Wade decision that had established a woman's right to a safe and legal abortion, adding that women who needed abortions thereafter, "Well, they perhaps will have to go … they'll have to go to another state."

I guessed he meant that 51st state in the sky where Supreme Court rulings would not apply.

Political absurdities converge with hotel absurdities, as one moves around the world. Such as, for example, no matter where, hotels have well understood how desperate guests can be for morning coffee, so the hotels either charge a fortune for even just one pot through room service, or install high-tech but incomprehensible coffee-makers in the rooms to help justify the room price. In my room was yet another fancy coffee-maker of a type I had not seen before, with so many moving parts a cup of coffee between an assembly line ordeal.

I did my best to contend, but all I accomplished was to set my espresso cup dancing and vibrating as the coffee machine strained to make the coffee and none dripped out. Perhaps I had put the capsule containing the coffee in backwards, but at least the cup had a good time.

I wasn't due anywhere until after lunch, so I decided to take a first morning walk. The sky was dazzlingly cobalt blue, and I walked to the nearest garden and waited for the sun to hit my bench. In Morocco it looks like it should be summer every day, but looks are a tease. Temperatures can be low even as the sun blazes and the sky takes your breath away.

I dozed off just for a bit and checked my watch. Time to engage.

I walked back and noticed the many soldiers standing around and how much military security was in the streets to guard all the climate change visitors and dignitaries. But the huge camouflage-patterned security jeep parked just a block from my hotel seemed to be guarding mainly the Louis Vuitton shop.

I changed clothes and headed to the hotel where my speaking engagement would be held. My task was to moderate a panel of experts on emerging new financial tools aimed at shifting capital toward clean energy investments. All the speakers knew their material cold, and it was inspiring to hear them bring the workings of money alive. Attendees came from all over the world, also exciting and perhaps one of the most important reason for these conferences to keep on going—despite its countless flaws, the UN remains the world's only official keeper of the dream of international collaboration to solve global problems.

The Moroccans entertain generously and we wrapped up our session with high-concept canapés and bubbly white wine. As always, I felt we'd both advanced and reversed—where would these new ideas land, who would take them forward, did this world of words make any difference to the climate change problem? Yes and no, I thought, as always.

I had no pass to enter the official UN Conference area, but through the grapevine of friends and colleagues I heard that the US delegation, which had triumphantly helped seal the deal that came to be known as the Paris Agreement the year before, at COP-21, was now funereal, given the election of Trump. I heard that the US delegation was being pumped non-stop for any information on whether Trump would stick with what in Paris had been so painstakingly won. I had been in Paris when the Agreement was signed, and it is true the mood there was euphoric, but I also knew that the world has been talking about addressing climate change since at least 1992 with very little progress to show. Now, here we were in Morocco, thousands of us, and the fragile consensus appeared to be hanging by a thread named Trump.

I felt sorry for the Moroccans, who had hoped to stamp their national brand on the Paris result and host an event that could be credited with advancing global will. But the US election had soured the hopes and it was hard to shake the despondency that came with the rise of Trump.

That night, though, Marrakech was due for a super-moon, when the full moon was due to look especially large and brilliant. After the worry about Trump, the super-moon was the next biggest topic of conversation. But the city's lights drowned out the super-size effect. The regular moon was only routinely gorgeous, gleamingly gold.

The night was perfect, crystal clear, and my obligations were behind me. Visions were dancing—I could see the tops of palm trees, smell the dates and even hear camel bells. But that picturesque cliché of Morocco was only the movie running in my head. I was staying in an upscale suburb outside the old city walls, and though Morocco and the Moroccans I met were the perfect hosts, I just was failing to connect with the place or the moment. I had no yen to explore, no drive to stay longer. I had dinner with colleagues and hung around the hotel the next morning until it was time to leave.

In less than 48 hours in Morocco, I was back into the revealing society of airports. My lounge laissez passer led to a VIP salon, which raised a question all too aligned with the times. Can a VIP room grow too small? Too many VIPs? Too few real ones?

People began to complain that the sandwiches were gone and there was no more milk for the coffee. Passengers have become so used to being called guests they have come to feel all a guest's entitlements, every whim indulged and comforts at any stop en route once reserved only for sultans and their entourages.

Even the Wi-Fi rebelled, its signals pinched and pulled and tugged at by the unruly VIPS like children pulling at a beard. Finally, no Wi-Fi at all.

Outside, the Kingdom of Kuwait plane dwarfed all the other jets on the tarmac. I overheard someone say it had never carried more than two passengers, ever.

There were more security checks before we boarded, with hand luggage splayed open and searched fold by fold, and I could picture the day when airport inspectors might actually slash open linings looking for slush funds or bombs, then fold up the tatters and re-assemble it all with a smile, as if it was normal to slash luggage and passengers would have no recourse.

It was obvious that Europeans and Americans were getting a free pass on the extra security as the police stopped only passengers from nations other than the US or the EU. I could also imagine that one day a demagogue would take over a place called Civil State 1, a nation that used to have a name until all nation names were deleted because people had grown fearful of being identified with any place or ethnicity.

I reached London again so quickly, Morocco was nearly erased.

Of course, the British had their own reasons to be anxious. The Brexit vote had startled the whole nation, both the Leavers and the Remainers, and now they both faced a precipice—no one could claim to know how Brexit would proceed and what it would cost.

Leaving Europe seemed so wrong for the British, so headed backward. I have come to love London and its global feel, its millipede public transport system, the Thames ferries, countless galleries and sumptuous gardens, fine formality and flip-hip bustle throwing off as much electricity as my beloved New York.

London had become a truly modern global cosmopolitan mecca and now this Brexit, this step away from unity, back to being an island. It seemed totally wrong for the time, to secede from world history's greatest peace project at a time of such global tension, and, of course, as wrong as the election of Trump.

I wandered around the next day with a friend, Marina, who had come to London for a visit from Germany. We walked and talked, catching up on our lives—she was as worried about the US election as I was. Europeans who remembered World War II simply could not digest either Brexit or Trump.

Marina and I wandered into the Serpentine Sackler Gallery to take in an exhibition of contemporary assemblage art by Helen Marten, who had won the Turner Prize. Marina and I had been so busy talking politics and trying to look at the art at the same time, that Marina wandered over a line of rope and the gallery guard freaked out—"You are in the art, you are in the art—move out, move out," the guard yelled. We both jumped away but then howled with laughter. How easy to transgress the boundaries of a work of art that needs to have an in/out sign.

I read later that the artist herself had worried a bit about how to keep traffic moving gamely around her installations in the narrow corridors of what had once been a gunpowder stock house.

We wandered some more, and went on to the Tate Modern to catch the photo collection of Elton John, who seemed to have ownership of among the most famous and images in the history of photography.

Marina would be leaving for home later that night, so I made one more call to the Old Vic to see if I could score a ticket to the sold-out performance of *King Lear* with the brilliant actress Glenda Jackson playing Lear. I had been trying twice a day for weeks, but just then, sitting in the window sill at the Tate while Marina looked at postcards, I managed it. That great British system of encouraging ticketholders who cancel to return their tickets for full refund means there is always a chance that a late ticket will materialize—a much better system than in the US where when you book a ticket they tell you at least twice that the ticket is non-refundable, non-changeable or non-usable if you don't make the show.

I was buoyant and there was still time to show Marina the extraordinary Nelson Stair at Somerset House, built originally in the 18th century and since restored, an architectural work of curves and lines both dizzying and delightful, that another friend had once introduced to me. We raced there to make it before the building closed, but I couldn't find the staircase.

We kept getting lost among waiters and waitresses who were catering a private party for a perfume-maker and none of them knew how to direct us to the Nelson Stair, though a few of them tried to find out by tapping their iPhone GPS with no luck. Finally, I asked a guard, who tried to explain the route and realized that words simply couldn't convey all the twists and turns and corridors we would need to follow.

"Come with me," he finally said. He, black, walked us out of the building, around the corner, and back in by another entrance and straight to the Nelson. I was so grateful and moved. Here, exactly why Trump's election was wrong and Brexit even more so. A man with a basic job as a guard, who could as easily let us go without his help, taking his work as a point of pride and doing a favor for perfect strangers. To me he epitomized the basic human elegance and decency that Trump's election had tried to dispel by setting one group against the other.

Marina loved the stairs and I savored their swirling design all over again too. It was the perfect end to our day. Marina flew back to Germany and I took the Tube to the theater.

At rush hour, the London Tubes are filled with trains that have just enough space between them, so often do they seem to arrive. Still on a busy night there can never be enough and the cars are always packed. Almost all the passengers were attached to their phones, either by hand or some bluetooth wire. The earphone of the passenger standing next to me leaked out sounds like a pan tossing sizzling eggs.

My last-minute theater seat was dead center, and as I inched down the row, I had the weird feeling I knew the woman who was seated next to me. At intermission we figured it out. We knew each other from New York, and had each gotten the last two tickets in yet another one of those coincidences in the roulette wheel of living that can only bring astonishment.

But we didn't dwell on it. The play was the thing. I had seen *Lear* before, but never like this. Putting her acting career on hold, Glenda Jackson had served more than 20 years in the UK Parliament, even running for Mayor of London, and she brought to the King truly vivid political drive and despair. Lear cared about the fate of his nation, not only his daughters. Maybe I had not paid enough attention to the play before, but I had not remembered the dying Lear as both despairing father and vanquished broken statesman.

When the performance ended, all the cast including Glenda Jackson appeared for the curtain call, and the demure British audience applauded fully but everyone remained seated. The curtain dropped but swayed.

Then, Glenda Jackson emerged alone. That was it. All of the sold-out Old Vic stood, applauding and even whistling. Oh, the moment of greatness at hand, the unadulterated power of a masterpiece played masterfully.

But Albany's last lines haunted me on the way out:

'The weight of this sad time we must obey;
Speak what we feel, not what we ought to say.
The oldest hath borne most: we that are young
Shall never see so much, nor live so long.'

I took a late-night brandy in the hotel bar alone. I felt blessed despite what I was trying to forget.

Chapter 3

La Pièce de Résistance

My lucky life continued to roll out. Besides the panel in Morocco, I had been asked to moderate similar dialogues in Paris and Amsterdam and so thanks to the brilliant Eurostar, it was off to the City of Light in less than three hours, a short slip across the Channel that had kept the Nazi army at bay for four years of blood and bombing that now we crossed as if just pinching Europe together between our thumb and forefinger. Or what had been Europe until June, 2016, and the Brexit vote to separate the UK from the same Europe it had spent the lives of a half a million soldiers and trillions in today's dollars to saving only a few decades earlier.

England was leaving the very Europe it had once moved heaven and earth to protect and for what purpose and to what end, not year clear. Trump had compared his upset victory to the Brexit upset. Two wrongs definitely do not make a right.

The perfect green and sienna-brown landscape rolled past, each *clickety-clack* swallowing scores of years of European history, battles and death and treaties and tenuous peace until, now, the European Union, shaky and in the news. If you just kept taking trains across Europe, you could cross a half a dozen different nations in one day.

Given the time change from London, I rolled into Paris backward, gaining an hour and changing time zone, money, language and memories with the click of the machine to 'composter' my ticket. Say "good-day and thanks" to the natty stewards and stewardesses who see you off at the track at St Pancras in London, then "bonjour et merci" as you step off to the French madames et messieurs who greet you at the Gare de Nord.

I headed back to my favorite digs on the rue Jacob, off rue St Benoit. How many times I had walked these streets, wet and shiny that night as they often were, narrow and quiet just off the Boulevard St Michel, through the familiar mahogany swinging doors. I had only a night here this time so resolved to be quick with the rituals.

I dropped off my bag and went down the street toward the Seine to have another look at the plaque. When the hotel receptionist had some time ago told me that there was a plaque down the street important for Americans to see, I had set out. The plaque became part of my Paris settling-in must list, but I've always taken its message for granted. This time, I almost yearned to read it again. There, indeed at the corner of the rue des St Peres, at 56 Rue Jacob, an engraved stone plaque states: *'In this building, formerly the York Hotel, on September 3, 1783, David Hartley, in the name of the King of England, Benjamin Franklin, John Jay, John Adams, in the name of the United States of America, signed the definitive treaty of peace recognizing the independence of the United States.'*

Only fairly recently, a French friend had booked us a detailed tour of Versailles and our guide, a French-born anglophile named Mr Smee, had taken special pride in pointing out to me, the lone American in the group, the very table where that Treaty had been signed, a table so precious it was now kept in the Palace of Versailles.

But all well and good to savor the table. What of the system it celebrated? Franklin himself had pinpointed the challenges. Reportedly, in 1787, after the Constitutional Convention had completed its work, James McHenry, a delegate from the state of Maryland, had asked Franklin his opinion of the result. "Well, doctor, what have we got," McHenry reportedly wondered, "a Republic or a monarchy?" Franklin had replied, "A republic—if you can keep it."

Given the Trump election, the question was back in play.

On the road, I always feel I'm living in two conditions, one of doing and one of thinking, between the thrill of fresh experience and the pluck of the absurd, of open eyes and yearning for habits. But, in the time of Trump, the travel zone had become more vexing and tense. I felt pressed between acting and opining, looking out beyond the days I was actually living. I just could not stay in the moment.

Even the Rue Jacob was deviating from the norms I knew. It was 6 a.m. and there were birds somewhere already waking up, but no coffee yet in the hotel. By the time the birds had hit the street before, I could always also hear the tinkle of cups in the cafes outside and the beginning of the morning. Was Paris slowing down?

After my Paris commitment, I was off again in a superlative train to Amsterdam, and the glow of the Amstel River lit as if through amber.

My eye caught the glint of chrome outside of the train station—the bike rack there looked like a gigantic game of jacks, silver spokes and wheels piled so high I wondered how long it would take to get your bike loose once you had put it in the rack.

My taxi driver complained about the bikes. Said he, "I used to love them and use them but now there are so many, the rest of us cannot get around." So maybe bike-friendliness can also go too far. I nearly got clipped by bike riders as I ambled around the canals.

I should have been walking faster anyway, for I was running late for dinner. I had taken to using my phone as a watch like so many others. But my phone had already had its Brexit—it had stayed on UK time for some reason.

No matter, though, for soon enough I was back in London again to get my flight home at last, a snap via local train from Amsterdam to Brussels, impeccable service and signage, all with passenger comfort and smooth sailing in mind.

I considered the contradictions of my state. What was I doing with two bookmarks in the same book, nearly 20 pens in my knapsack and no shortages ahead? I had too much of everything. And the world too, where hotels have become so deluxe, so gadget fixated, I have become too stupid to know how to turn on the TV. Meanwhile I woke again to news of Trump belittling just about everything done by President Obama.

On the plane home, the reality again seeped in to every open thought channel and I relived my conclusions. My doubts about Hillary's winning had begun mid-summer, because I never felt her gaining momentum on her own, only in relationship to Trump's errors, his "you can grab them by the pussy" moment becoming her high point when a recording from some years earlier had surfaced, catching Trump's crude derision of women. And, as the song's lament goes, 'is that all there is'? There was no juice to her story, no buzz in Scranton, with dedicated geeks devoted to computerized lists and an inflated sense of their value.

On the other hand, my mind told me, do not forget she won the popular vote. The east and west coasts, where Hillary had won, had become the bookends of American democracy, and now the year was ending with the lamentable inescapable truth of the election results. What was the path of resistance that fit this occasion? How would I know?

Usually, I love to ring in midnight with friends, but this year I knew I would not be happy singing *Auld Lang Syne* as if no shock had occurred. Where to go where the words, and the world, might seem truly new?

Chapter 4

The Sky of in Between

I looked at the map. If the world was my lover, then why not look there for comfort. Such a beautiful swath of puzzle pieces, vast plates torn apart by thundering ancient geological forces and always seeming to try to push themselves back together again. The map looked like I felt.

Where to go?

Come to South Africa, anytime, a friend Alison had invited just under a year before, when candidate Trump was still nearly a laughing stock among the pundits and those who thought they knew. She had been an activist in the protest period of the 1980s and 90s against apartheid, and was a deep and eloquent devotee of her homeland. Her passion for South Africa was infectious, and so I wrote her a tentative email. Was a New Year's visit remotely feasible—did that qualify for anytime? Overnight came her welcome. I moved again into trip-planning gear.

The Cape of Good Hope on New Year's Day seemed like the perfect place for new beginnings.

The trip started as all my trips do, with buying a book of the place ahead, this time Nadine Gordimer, who had written *The Pick-Up* when pens and paper met like friends on the journey, not the zap-zap of today's brain swipe. But even digital time would have trouble keeping up with what I had in mind. I was about to take on three continents, staying away for as long and as far as I could.

Again, I took the day flight to London and flew over on Christmas Eve. Still, the flight was packed with not a single empty seat. Less than six hours after flying the Atlantic and ten hours from when my alarm clock had woken me, including time to check in, admire the hotel Christmas tree and have my usual bowl of soup and glass of claret for late-arrival dinner, I was crossing the threshold of St Patrick's in slightly seedy Soho Square. Maybe this was Jack the Ripper's church, I thought, as I stepped inside.

Christmas Eve services were about to begin, and my scenario of the new had begun to unfold. I wanted to hear new voices grasping for the common voice of Christmas carols.

I lit a candle for my mother at the church's large nativity set, with its donkeys and cows and camels and shepherds and Joseph and Mary all in place, all waiting for the newborn Christ-child to appear. My mother had loved nativities, and I took my seat just as I heard the last *rat-tat-tat* of shoes hitting the stone steps as the altar attendants and the choir rushed into the church to be in place on time.

St Patrick's is known for welcoming worshippers from all walks of life and background, whether needing solace from a need or a vice.

But that night, all was calm, all was bright. In the pews, there were people who seemed to come from all over the world, skin tones from ebony to paper white, pasty and swarthy, turbaned and bald, some men in long white beards like the froth of Victoria Falls. There was standing room only by the time the service started.

I had been raised in the Catholic Church and then abandoned weekly mass and all but the major spectacles at an early age, though my love for Christmas carols has never waned, the same melodies familiar to so many and sung in any language. But this audience of singers was having trouble staying together; the organist at St Patrick's played at a lagging pace. Some people gave up singing and just hummed, including me, but that served the same purpose. A joyful sense of union began to hold the room.

Still, the priest seemed stern for a Christmas Eve when he started his homily—I figured he did not think much of our singing but was soldiering on. When he took to the pulpit hundreds of eyes were glued to him and hanging on his every word, but as soon as he deviated from his congratulations at the birth of Christ, and made the comment that that 65% of the people in the UK had "no abiding belief in God", people started shifting around and a vibe of discomfort suddenly ran through the crowd.

Maybe the priest felt it too, because he tempered his scolding tone and moved on to the problems of the world. He declared that "because we do not adore God" debacles occur. He cited homelessness, and the vicious wars in Syria and Somalia as examples. He may have been proselytizing on the back of Christmas joy, but he was right about the social crises that seemed to worsen before the eyes of the world. Do not look away, he seemed to implore.

Then, he ended his remarks and we moved back to full church Christmas carol mode. *O Come All 'Ye Faithful* was next, and this time, led by him, sung at a pace we could hang onto. Now no one hummed but all sang in full-throated English with all kinds of accents coming through, clipping this or that word or stretching it out. We melted into more or less a chorus. We sat down and stood up in unison, slipping in more Christmas carols between prayers, according to cues given by the deacon.

The church was overflowing as the service hit its holiest mid-point, and the priest reminded those who were not Roman Catholic or had been away from Mass for a long time that they should not receive Communion, but any and all were welcome to seek a blessing, which amounted to a slight touch on the cheek from him.

I hadn't realized that the Communion host is no longer placed delicately on the communicant's tongue by the priest, but rather into the communicant's hands for him or her to place. I figured this must be a new public health measure to keep the priest's hands out of people's mouths, but it seemed demeaning to the occasion because of the sloppy way some people were sopping up the thin wafer meant to symbolize the body and blood of Christ, seeming to swallow it right then and there, even chew it—completely forbidden when I was growing up.

My eyes remained fixed on the priest and the prayer book, and I caught the altar boys moving off the altar and behind me only out of the corner of my eye.

As I left when the service ended, reminded by the priest to take a look at the nativity crèche, there in the cradle was the newborn baby, to my surprise. I hadn't seen the altar boys or anyone put him there, and so I smiled at the thought that therefore the birth could still count as a miracle to me.

The night was freezing, but at the end of the service, the priest lingered on the sidewalk outside, saying good night to everyone after asking us where we all came from. It was a potpourri of places—from Brooklyn to Pakistan, and who can imagine what brought us all to that little corner on Soho Square where usually all-night carousers fall down drunk on the curbstones. There were no drunks that night—and I walked the few steps home buoyantly as if relaunched.

****

Christmas Day morning found me snug in my room, looping trickles of honey into my porridge, a crimson miniature poinsettia on my tray. Who could have been luckier?

Outside, the silent day followed the silent night, except for the futile peck-peck of pigeons on the empty sidewalk. No one had told them that even the all-night denizens of Dean Street stay home on Christmas Eve and so there were no crumbs or tossed out chicken wings left from the eat-and-sleep-on-the-street usual Soho crowd.

Still, I could pick up the now-and-then scent of urine when I took a little morning walk—Soho is never quite without itself.

On Christmas Day London is like a tomb, with no tube, no Heathrow Express, no buses and no way to the airport except a taxi that can nevertheless make exceptionally quick time on the roads nearly empty of traffic. Christmas in the UK can be dead as a doornail, other than in Chinatown, where the only restaurants are open and offer dim sum galore to the many visitors in London who for whatever reason are not sitting down to a Christmas roast.

Me, I went to the airport early and had light finger sandwiches for lunch at the British Airways lounge, where champagne flows so freely, those who seem not to be used to it drink more than what might be called for at the hour of the day.

I was using up some airline miles for part of the trip and so settled myself into BA Club World, once known as business class before airlines started masking the class system and giving economy a name just as pretentious. The airlines have cooked up a batch of amazing euphemisms for the back of the plane, like 'espace' or 'main'. On BA, it was 'traveler' for economy but in Ireland the term can be used as an even more derogatory term than 'gypsy' and I wondered if BA knew. My metaphor wheel began turning as the 'travelers' wandered into the plane. Just like real-life outside, I thought, where people are essentially being made to walk through the business class of life, seeing right before their eyes what others have that they do not.

And yet, aha, there were rows 1-4, cut off from even us in business class, even more rarified and cloistered, even more upfront, behind an accordion gray wall, like a head blocked off from the chest during thoracic surgery—first class, up there, separated from us all.

My seat required a three-ply folded information card to explain all the comforts the seat had to offer, including its memory foam headrest. If you are going to pamper people, might as well overdo it, I thought, though I doubted that most in the cabin were actually paying full fare. There were too many infants and children in business class to be other than freebies, and too many were excited with the gadgets, with too much oohing and ahing at every little perk and all too loud by far.

Talk about class warfare. What if one day the airlines found themselves with a revolt of the paying passengers on their hands—the paying 1% against the non-paying 99%. And what about just making the plane more comfortable for everyone, push up the average, and abandon classes altogether?

Now I was planning a single payer system for airline travel, munching on pre-take off salted nuts. Easy for me to complain about perks on a plane I had earned only by flying on other planes.

Many airlines have a truly sumptuous business class, but the BA system was trying to have it both ways. The business cabin was too large and seats were packed together in a weird zigzag fashion so we had to jump inelegantly over each other's feet if we wanted to leave our seats, tripping like tipsy gazelles on stray blankets or headphone wires or extra-long legs.

To offer the privacy and isolation from the crowds for which we were, in theory, paying, each seat had a room divider, and my seatmate, whose eyes met mine in a moment of disgust at the thought we would be eye-to-eye all night, need not have worried. As soon as we took off, it was okay to raise the divider and I was glad too. My seatmate soon disappeared into his own room, zipped away from me and everyone else. In business class we had been given a way to buy our way free of each other, the airplane equivalent of Trump's anti-immigrant wall.

But even with the divider, the ultra-privacy of the cabin was not so private. The seat designers had been skimpy and we could see each other's video and laptop screens, and the cabin soon became a tent of flickering lights.

In this set-up, the stewards and stewardesses have become chief caterers, their proud cabin service now the equivalent of babysitting.

One stewardess flirted over my head and the room divider to the fellow on the other side of my wall. Anything could happen behind the translucent glass as we flew through the night, I imagined, as the stewardess handed him his third glass of champagne in less than half an hour.

Back to the election. I was watching an interview with Neil de Grasse Tyson, the indefatigable astrophysicist and defender of the U.S space program and all its cosmic radiance and down-to-earth spin-off innovations. He gave the quote of the day as far as I was concerned, to the question of whether he had been asked to join the Trump Administration: "As long as I don't work for the President, then the President works for me."

I declined dinner in favor of getting a good night's sleep and with no time change between London and South Africa, it was a normal night for my body.

I settled into my pod, between Christmas and its end, my seatmate and me, sleeping the only slim line between the continent of Europe and the continent of Africa ahead, leaving almost all study of it aside until I would arrive there and, in the meantime, this timbre of in between—taking off exactly on time from London at 8:30 p.m., latitude and longitude like rubber bands in my hands, west-east and now north to as far south as one can go in Africa. My odyssey had truly begun though, as I finally closed my eyes, I had no idea whatsoever where we could be.

Chapter 5

Rolihlahla

Even though I had been a somewhat cranky brat on the plane, I know when to be grateful, and I was superlatively grateful for what would happen next.

Not only had Alison invited me to come, she had arranged for me to be met at the Johannesburg airport and well taken care of during the long layover for my next flight to her home in Cape Town. I, big shot world traveler, had actually booked myself to the wrong city in my haste to escape the Trump result, and then could not change when I discovered my error. So I had nearly a day's wait in Johannesburg.

Still, blessings definitely came along one after the other. Alison knew a fine gentleman taxi driver in Johannesburg who took me under his wing. She had designed the itinerary: "Please pick her up, take her to the Apartheid Museum, wait for her, and then take her back to the airport."

First things first. In Johannesburg, first things means the story of apartheid, that ugly violent system of official sanctioned segregation that had prevailed in South Africa for half a century and finally collapsed in 1990.

The driver, John, black African and tall, was right on time, and my first sights of South Africa were routine, no savannahs or rambling veldt as we hit the modern highway. John and I made small talk until he suddenly skillfully swerved to miss an oncoming truck that had been headed right at us. "Must have fallen asleep," he observed coolly. "His plate was from Durban—that's a long way, a long night."

Drivers know so much more than the roads, always.

With pride, he pointed out the soccer stadium in sight and I responded with unfounded glee. Who did not know the mighty story of how Nelson Mandela, South Africa's crowning hero and its first post-apartheid President, had led the country to thundering pride at the soccer stadium when the South African rugby team, the Springboks, won the Rugby World Cup in 1995. The team had been deeply racist during apartheid, but eventually embraced Mandela as their leader thanks to his non-stop reconciliation effort. His inspiration and nationalist zest for rugby led the Springboks to victory and their win had helped knit together the fractured country. Mandela had been expert at spreading the power of his peacemaking to build coalitions with those who would have just as soon spit on him not so long before he became President. Morgan Freeman had played Mandela in the movie *Invictus*, about the Springboks, which I had seen. Now we were driving past the site, or so I thought.

But John, not wanting me to feel the wrong emotions, had to say, "No, not *that* stadium. This is just a regular one."

We made good time to the Museum, arriving about an hour before opening. But already open for business right nearby was a gambling casino and hotel, Gold Reef City. I said to John, "Let's see if we can get something to eat."

We parked. It was surreal to spend waiting time in a casino offering slot machines for breakfast, but that is what we did. John told me he had never been inside—"I've only dropped people off." But with me, he wandered in and ordered coffee, as if my white skin were his passport. Racial separation still holding on, but then gone again. As it turned out, almost all the customers inside were black and it was me, the only white, too early for the museum.

The casino had been built in 1995 to generate jobs, and the casino developers had also committed to building the museum, though no casino revenue goes to the museum.

John and I had coffee together and then it was time. I approached the museum with what I thought was a genuine curiosity, but I soon realized was just the mundane curiosity of an outsider still living in theory.

I had done my share of boycotting in the late 1980s and 90s of the apartheid regimes, refusing to buy any products from South Africa, and attended all the plays of the staunch apartheid opponent Athol Fugard that came through New York City, and, didn't I have my Gordimer with me?

But what did I know. Nothing at all. What could I possibly know about the depth of the venom apartheid inflicted? Now, though, I would get my traveler's dose.

When you pay your admission to enter the museum, designed by a consortium of local and international architects and opened in 2001, your ticket is stamped with one of the basic categories that used to apply: 'Blankes=Whites'; or 'Nie Blankes=NonWhites'. I had to smile that the Afrikaans word for 'whites' had us sounding like blanks.

And so the visitor enters the museum through a sickening labyrinth intended to invoke the experience of apartheid using lanes that correspond to category and skin color, each separated from the other by an opaque wall, with lists of what you could do and not do in that lane, all the things allowed or denied you because, and only because, of your category. The category stamped on your ticket was as random as your draw at birth.

Total immersion and a quick lesson. If anyone wondered how apartheid worked, now they knew. Separation and delineation from your very exit from the birth canal, so much enforced separation and signs that proclaimed 'no blacks' here, 'whites only'. According to one museum exhibition of photos, there were eventually so many signposts crowded with signs proclaiming rules that even the South African public, black and white, could often not tell which signs applied.

When had all this begun?

Perhaps as early as the 15th century, when the Portuguese had mapped the South African coast as they searched incessantly for a short trade route to Asia via Africa. This brought the Dutch and the British too, who eventually came to dominate the African trading routes between Europe and the fabled riches of the East. In 1652, the Dutch established a primary foothold in Cape Town to serve the expanding Dutch East India Company need for a fuel and food stopover station for their ships.

Racial discrimination was entwined with these earliest trade rivalries, as each succeeding or competing Western power displaced or enslaved the local indigenous people such as the San, Bantu, Nguni and Khoikhoi, who lived either as pastoral farmers or hunter-gatherers with distinct social and cultural civilizations and structures of their own, and who had been masters of their own lands for decades and were dispersed across north, south, east and west of South Africa.

Eventually western colonialists imported more slaves and indentured servants from Muslim areas, India and South Asia, and this led to racial mixing of many variations. Still, white Europeans remained all-powerful, gradually expanding their hold on the land and its agriculture, wildlife and, in the late 1800s, with the discovery gold and diamonds, and mineral resources as well.

From the outset, though, resistance to racial repression existed, including as early as 1510 when Portuguese settlers tried to kidnap local Khoikhoi children in the Cape Town area, triggering a Khoikhoi uprising, and the Khoikhoi kept the Portuguese at bay for a time.

But the South African region steadily evolved into several Western spheres of influence and colonies and the riches of South African ignited bitter bloody rivalries. Wars in Europe between the British, Dutch and French transferred to Africa, and continuous warfare ensued, soon also embroiling also the Xhosa-speaking indigenous black people who lived in the Eastern Cape.

Meanwhile, chafing under British incursions and rejecting the British emancipation of slaves in 1834, farmers descended from the original Dutch, German and French colonialists, known as the Boers, trekked into the north and east regions to make their own way and their own whites-only rule. By the mid-1800s, white settlements were everywhere in the South Africa region—what became known as the Afrikaner movement—and despite their constant resistance, black and colored people were relegated to underdog status in all forms. As early as 1853 in the Boer Republic that covered the Transvaal area, only white people were allowed to vote and own property and black people were expected to work for them. Pass laws, too, existed then, as early as 1866 in Transvaal, and any black person found outside the permissible residential area without a pass from an employer, magistrate, missionary, military commander or principal tribal chief could be arrested.

People from India, too, were objects of racial discrimination, drawing the young Mahatma Gandhi, who was practicing law in South Africa at the time, into two decades of protest and struggle to establish rights for Indian South Africans. The Boers sought to remain independent, which the British could not abide, and so in 1899, the second vicious Anglo-Boer war broke out in which the British dispatched half a million soldiers to crush about 65,000 Boers, with each side dragging in local black populations as draftees, wagon drivers and cannon fodder. In a notorious and horrific blaze of brutality, the British General Kitchener adopted scorched earth warfare and set up concentration camps—about 26,000 Boer women and children and 14,000 black and colored people died. The Boers gave up, but only reinforced their whites-only preferences.

The Union of South Africa came into existence in 1910, pulling together the regions and main four colonial areas, but allowing home rule, including rights for whites only, to stand. The role black people had played to support colonial armies, and their losses and suffering as victims of those armies and decades of turmoil was neither recognized nor compensated. In 1913 the Land Act was passed, segregating blacks by territory, forcing them into reserves and blacks-only settlements, reserving 90% of the la. for whites.

To resist and protest this ongoing repression, the South African Native National Congress was formed in 1912, renamed later the African National Congress (ANC), bringing together black tribal leaders and progressive whites. They formed a coalition and headed to London to make a plea for British assistance in reversing discriminatory land practices and rights restrictions, to no avail. Strikes, demonstrations, uprisings and bloody confrontations continued.

In 1944, the ANC founded its Youth League, and in 1948 its Women's League to recognize women's leadership in the resistance. But also in 1948, the pro-Afrikaaner National Party came into power in South Africa, including lingering pro-Nazi sympathizers in its ranks. Gradually, with the accession to leadership of extremists Daniel F. Malan and H. F. Verwoeld, the party turned the fragmented rules, attitudes and decades of racial repression and discrimination into official national policy—codified and explicit and known as apartheid.

The bitterness left among the white settlers in South Africa after the Boer War is clear from the Johannesburg museum's early rooms, and its connection to the rise of apartheid equally clear. The British had delivered poison to the Afrikaners, who then delivered even more poison to the Africans, who had also been tortured and murdered by the British. Vicious cycles: give people the heel and they give it to the next person. We were living this right now in the United States—had not Trump primed his raw base with the idea that America could be forever prosperous if we just expelled all the 'others' and closed the door behind us?

But apartheid was worse than economic walls—it was walls between hearts, brains, between every kindness and decent instinct with which we presume to be born.

'Apartheid' means 'apartness' in Afrikaans, the main language that evolved among the original Afrikaner settlers. Indeed, the official apartheid pass system divided South Africans into four main groups: European, Asiatic, Coloured and Bantu. Bantu was further subdivided into eight groups. There were countless categories and all rights and all services were dictated by the pass—from voting rights to ambulance service, schools to roads, buses to bathrooms to birth and death certificates, where you could live, work, whom you could marry—all defined by genetic background, skin color and tightness of the curl of the hair. This infrastructure of hated identity passbooks supported the whole architecture of apartheid.

I was not proud to be carrying my whites-only ticket.

Then through the winding museum itself, brilliantly designed so there is a gradual but unforgiving immersion in the build-up, rituals and resistance to apartheid.

Then came the first panels on Nelson Mandela. I read that his tribal name had been Rolihlahla—which means pulling the branch of a tree, or the one who disturbs the established order—a name given to him at birth. I winced at the poignant prescience of it—pull he did, and what tree and what order.

Then the beginnings of the price paid for freedom. Numerous tapes of the young lawyer Mandela, who had become Secretary of the ANC Youth League in 1944, movingly and eloquently making his anti-apartheid stance, including films and newsreels of beatings and shootings and protests, always luminous black skin shining as if oiled, intoxicatingly beautiful compared to the dull pudgy faces of the white overlords.

Mandela projected super-human dignity in even the most antiquated black-and-white film print. He narrated a film about masculinity and young men, explaining the circumcision ritual and how tribal men had to find their strength in enduring the pain. He had himself endured the rite, but he did not have a breath of brag in his voice. I began to cry at his softness, his forgiving tones.

What strength in the man, Herculean in its way compared to the heavy, ugly, armored people-crusher vehicles used by the apartheid police, also displayed, and the replica minuscule prison cells on Robben Island, just off the harbor in Cape Town, where Mandela and other resistance heroes such as Walter Sisulu, Ahmed Kathrada and many other famous and nameless anti-apartheid heroes had been imprisoned, tortured and confined in solitary for decades and left to die. Women too, like Albertina Sisulu and Winnie Mandela, also protested, got arrested, protested again, got shot and killed, lost their children to police reprisals or exile.

At Robben Island, despite its horrors, Mandela worked and wrote his letters, resisting every form of indignity, apparently even once wryly introducing one of his rare visitors to his jailer as 'my chief honor guard'. Who knows how he survived and endured through so many years of struggle that, gradually, drew the support and solidarity of the world.

Mandela spoke out from prison through secret communications and began discussions on his release with Prime Minister Botha in 1986. When

Botha imposed conditions, Mandela refused, choosing to remain in prison. The world heard that news when Mandela's daughter read a letter from her father to a crowd in Soweto stadium. Pressure built on the apartheid overlords from within and without. Then Botha was replaced by de Klerk, and Mandela took up communications with the new Prime Minister, urging the idea of a multi-racial democracy to replace the hated and hateful apartheid system.

The costs of apartheid? Incalculable. Billions in lost and wasted human and social capital through half a century at least of vicious, racist, bloody social division; chronic under-education of non-white South Africans who were uprooted and resettled to separate enclaves and left to despair, unable to acquire skills, land or dignity; the strengths and budget of government diverted and squandered by the apartheid obsession with maintaining a vicious police and militarized state; and decades of international condemnation as a pariah state. Apartheid was a roster of horrors.

But then, like a tree riddled with decades of molded fungus and holes of rot, the tree fell, as if by a single shaft of wind. Mandela and de Klerk, the last Prime Minister of the apartheid period, negotiated tirelessly and then, it was over. The South African apartheid government declared the end. I entered the room filled with the films and newsreels that had recorded the fall of apartheid in full public view.

In a two-minute speech to the South African Parliament and the world, de Klerk declared Mandela would be released unconditionally and that as of that day, February 2, 1990, as of that moment, the ANC was no longer banned, the Communist Party was no longer banned either. All that had been banned was un-banned, and all that tormented South Africa was declared officially and forever ended, without any home or lingering acceptable advocate.

In resistance, once the tumbler starts to tumble, it cannot be stopped.

But the museum makes clear—so much blood was shed before the final anti-apartheid opening, so many boycotts led to so many prison cells and escapes—and where was the rest of the world while this poisoned world got built up? It suited so many to let apartheid last.

While I was watching de Klerk's transformational speech, I coughed and missed key statements—that's how few words he took to end apartheid. I had to watch the film again to get it all. So quickly did de Klerk drop the bans, his tongue must have felt on fire.

But then the slower burn, the numerous videos of testimony of so many who had been imprisoned and tortured or left for dead; statement after vivid statement given to the Truth and Reconciliation Commission that had been convened in 1994 as keeper of the public record of the shameful history of apartheid so that no one, not in South Africa or anywhere, could forget it, or dare to repeat it. I listened to a few witnesses, again with that idiotic tourist perspective, until I really opened my ears, really put myself in that time, and then I could not remain. The stories were too hard, too violent, and too honest.

I wandered around, losing my way at times, drifting forward and backward in time, skipping a panel or exhibit only to find I had to go back—now that I was here, why was I skipping? I gave myself over to the effect of the museum.

I compared the superficiality of what I had known about the South African struggle to the volumes of knowledge I was taking in. New scenario all right. All this was new.

But never far from any corner, Mandela's flashing irresistible smile. His heart was shining every time he spoke it seemed to me. I was glued to a lively interview toward the end of his Presidency, when he was asked about his wearing a bowtie every day, to which he replied with a twinkle, that after he left office, "I will never wear a bowtie again."

What a feeling for the man. And accolades everywhere when he left prison; smiling thousands, gifts in every form, including a superb bright red Mercedes convertible from the workers of Mercedes South Africa, their homage.

But, also, quietly but inescapably, the sublime Constitution of the new South Africa, proclaiming the end of apartheid forever through the new beginning of justice and fairness—a rock-solid document, crystal clear, forgiving of history, and radiant with hope:

'Preamble

We, the people of South Africa,
Recognise the injustices of our past;
Honour those who suffered for justice and freedom in our land;
Respect those who have worked to build and develop our country; and
Believe that South Africa belongs to all who live in it, united in our diversity.

We therefore, through our freely elected representatives, adopt this Constitution as the supreme law of the Republic so as to:

Heal the divisions of the past and establish a society based on democratic values, social justice and fundamental human rights;

Lay the foundations for a democratic and open society in which government is based on the will of the people and every citizen is equally protected by law;

Improve the quality of life of all citizens and free the potential of each person; and

Build a united and democratic South Africa able to take its rightful place as a sovereign state in the family of nations.

May God protect our people.

Nkosi Sikelel' iAfrika. Morena boloka setjhaba sa heso.

God seën Suid-Afrika. God bless South Africa.

Mudzimu fhatutshedza Afurika. Hosi katekisa Afrika.'

The document then went on to say:

'Republic of South Africa is one, sovereign, democratic state founded on the following values:

a. Human dignity, the achievement of equality and the advancement of human rights and freedoms.

b. Non-racialism and non-sexism.

c. Supremacy of the constitution and the rule of law.

d. Universal adult suffrage, a national common voters roll, regular elections and a multi-party system of democratic government, to ensure accountability, responsiveness and openness.'

And that all rights specified belong to everyone and that all citizens were:

'a. equally entitled to the rights, privileges and benefits of citizenship; and
b. equally subject to the duties and responsibilities of citizenship.
c. National legislation must provide for the acquisition, loss and restoration of citizenship.'

How sturdy and perfect—the infinite arc of the word 'everyone'.

And how much it meant to the people here then. They gave so much blood to create it—whereas back at home in the US we had just put the protection of our Constitution in the hands of a man who bragged about grabbing women in their most intimate parts and then laughed off his remarks as mere "locker room talk".

But South Africa too had its turn at such buffoonery. All was not well in the democracy Mandela had bequeathed. Jacob Zuma, also an anti-apartheid fighter who had been imprisoned with Mandela, once a true hero to his people and President of South Africa since 2009, was then clinging to power against thousands who wanted to see him out of office, fed up with the corruption and economic stagnation of his leadership and the continuing cracks in the dream that was once post-apartheid South Africa—Mandela's South Africa that had had to, at some point, move beyond him, majestic figure that he was.

I had been at the museum for two hours, though it felt so much longer, but I had that plane to catch. My fingers trembled still a bit as we returned to the car, as if a whirlwind of what I had not known had passed through my hands. What was my search for a path to resistance compared to what I had just seen?

On the way out of the parking lot, I spotted three black men standing on the side of the road, watching the cars pass by. What are they thinking, I had to wonder.

Soon it was back to the cacophony of the airport. A young woman with wavy hair like black wet streamers wore a heavy satin overskirt that made her look like a walking theater curtain. She pushed a luggage cart built it seemed to haul a refrigerator—boxes and bags, loaded with coming, going, giving, selling and, above all, shopping.

Then, a man in a butler's uniform spotted me, perhaps accustomed to people and categories, I concluded.

"Club over here, madam," he pointed directing me to where I should be. He was the maître d'hôtel of the lounge. Boom. That separation again, as if I had been about to wander out of a whites-only area by mistake. He guided me to where my ticket said I belonged in the mirror of the economic categories of the airport.

I milled around, at last drank some water, and took a thin nap, the hours on planes now beginning to weigh, eyes half closed, my mind still alert enough to be aware of time passing.

I spent most of the flight to Cape Town reconsidering the museum and its embodiment of courage.

And then, Cape Town, my first real steps in southern Africa that were not in transit. The airport hummed and bustled and was full of beautiful black people, each skin tone different, a color palette of ebony and amber and cream.

Separation had not at all gone away at home, and I eyed the Africans around me with the same envy of their grace I had felt as a white child in the era of school bussing when the new black children who entered our school were more well-dressed and well-spoken than the rest of us, not to mention as smart, if not smarter. Bussing, however controversial, cracked into our fear of the other and I am forever grateful.

And it is not as though we at home had not had a long history with our own form of apartheid. In 1910, for example, the city of Baltimore was only one of many US cities to install racially restrictive land and property ownership covenants. The Baltimore ordinance said: '*That no Negro may take up residence in a block within the city limits of Baltimore wherein more than half the residents are white. That no white person may take up his residence in such a block wherein more than half the residents are Negroes. That whenever building construction is commenced in a new city block the builder or contractor must specific in his application for a permit for which race the proposed house or houses are intended.*'

It was not until 1948 in the Shelley v. Kraemer case that the US Supreme Court struck down the power of state courts to uphold or enforce such racial land covenants, citing the Constitution's 14th Amendment protection from the denial of rights to any person by the States—at least that counterweight to apartheid that had come into existence the same year. But, still, not until 1961 did the Supreme Court take the position that the 14th Amendment also negated the legality of acts of private discrimination. That crucial decision could be rickety, I knew, as Trump's alt-right leanings imbued his likely nomination of judges to the Supreme Court and lower courts as well.

Soon enough, Alison picked me up and we headed off along the ribbon coast. Alison knew her city by heart and poured it out with zest, delight and perspective. She had spearheaded a research group to study and advocate for equitable policies to speed digital communications technology throughout Africa. She was constantly on the move, pushing and pulling progress and she was a fountain of observations of Africa past and present.

Very soon we were dominated by Cape Town's signature landscape feature, Table Mountain, a spectacular flat high sheet of stone that seemed to me the stone equivalent of a symphony whose tones had once been roaring but had been patted down by the palm of the conductor until the orchestra played as one. Table Mountain was one long legato note, the icon called simply The Mountain, to live around, walk around, and contemplate from any and all distances.

And on the sea side, as tiny as The Mountain is large, a wisp of land barely visible, infamous Robben Island, a smudge of light on the otherwise flat blue sheet, a permanent commentary and reference point, speaking back to the land, back to the bastions.

Still, even as the landscape thundered around us, there was no escaping the new American reality I embodied.

"So how is it?" Alison had asked as soon as we were in the car, a master at discussing politics even while driving and pointing out the curves of The Mountain. It was as if I had gotten a disease.

Being on the road as an American since the Trump election meant I now represented something that I found repugnant, yet made me a potential billboard of the America we had become. I was not at all used to trying to explain the new America Trump's election seemed to bring out of the shadows.

"It feels sickening," was my answer.

We reached Alison's flat and I settled into this my latest version of home away from home. We spent the evening over a lazy lovely meal, doors open to the sultry evening temperature of the southern hemisphere summer.

Alison's mother had been a prominent actress, theater producer and anti-apartheid activist, strongly influencing Alison, and their struggle and resistance had been essentially lifelong. I realized that part of what I had come for was to examine those pathways, reconnect with how others had met the wheels of power that killed, maimed and tortured while so much of the world looked on. Resisting the civil disintegration that had brought Trump to the Presidency was a garden walk by comparison to defeating apartheid, of course, and yet I began to feel stronger just by association. Or was I trying to infuse my confused ideas about what to do with the clarity I saw in the lives of others? I had told myself I was trying to rediscover my path to resistance, but was I, instead, trying to confess a sin?

History can come in doses too large for those of us trying to swallow it— 16 years had passed since Nelson Mandela's release from Robben Island, but global respect and admiration for him only seemed to grow with the passage of time. Trump, on the other hand, seemed to shrink in stature with each passing day. Insults to our democracy at home were piling up. Trump was scornful of the basic conflict of interest requirements expected of elected officials. Even given the ultra-private nature of his business holdings and the sticky ties to his children, Trump was still defiantly resisting any call that he divest himself of his personal assets or put them in a blind trust while he remained President as all recent Presidents of means had done. Nor was he willing to follow their precedents of releasing his tax returns, still vowing he never would.

And, while so many societies across the globe were trying to take hope from the "peace on earth" message that comes along with the holiday season which, this year, had Hanukkah and Christmas overlapping for the first time in three decades, Trump was fueling the nuclear fire with a macho boast on the much-watched MSNBC show, *Morning Joe*: "Let it be an arms race. We will outmatch them at every pass and outlast them all," he boasted.

How much of this litany did I have to own, or take the blame for? And how much could I reassure people who worried about the emergence of an America that was so far from the America they recognized, despite our faults.

If the people of South Africa now felt betrayed by the ANC, the party of Mandela, I felt betrayed by the whole party system at home, degraded in the recent election into a parade of primaries on the one hand, that produced 16 Republican candidates all too weak or scared to vanquish Trump, one of whom even stooped to letting him compare the size of their hands to their penises. And, on the other hand, only one viable candidate in the Democratic party who campaigned as if anointed and was unable to throw out ideas so exciting and appealing that fence-sitting Trump voters would have had to fall over to her side, no contest.

I explained these electoral and campaign faults to Alison and her various friends, black and white, to whom she had introduced me, most of whom were still agape and aghast at Trump's election, even as they had their own embarrassments, such as Jacob Zuma having proclaimed he had no fear of getting AIDS because he always took a shower after sex, promoting his own personal transmission of virus theory that would surely have been news to the virus.

I began to realize how much America was still on a pedestal—we had still such a reserve of good will, and Trump's election was draining it empty.

Even with all our sordid forays into Iraq and Vietnam, people still seemed astonished that we, the people of America, could have elected as crass and incompetent a man as Donald Trump, and I knew I was avoiding my home story by living another.

On my first full day in South Africa, we took an orientation walk along the Sea Point promenade, 11 kilometers long and bustling with so many people coming and going, it may have easily been a moving sidewalk, the blue sea behind, waves ruffling in, a few hearty swimmers cavorting on rocks slippery with oozing green kelp, laughing and chasing each other.

It was perfect summer weather, while the temperature was hovering around freezing back home, and I let loose my love of summer indulgence in shorts and a tee shirt, arms swinging as I stepped along, carrying nothing, trying to think nothing too.

That was not easy with Alison, whose erudite answer to my every lightweight question easily begat another. We chatted non-stop.

The promenade was precisely the melting pot I had expected of Cape Town, a magnet that pulled black and white and turbanned men and hajibed women to it, all drawn to the relaxed spirit of days off and the holiday season at the shore.

The place was packed two days after Christmas and we had kept up a healthy pace. It was time for a drink.

We stepped up to a fresh fruit juice bar operated by a lanky black woman wearing a tee shirt of bright orange and black and a wraparound silky black skirt. She managed three customers at once and her shop offered such an array of juices it took a while to take in the full menu. I fell back on the familiar and ordered a medium orange juice. I hadn't caught the lilt when she had spoken and misheard her when she had said she was out of OJ. She smiled and waited while I thought again. I had carrot juice and mint instead, with ginger. It was absolutely delicious and cool. But what impressed me was the good-natured patience she showed me as I bumbled through my simple order. Why had I expected otherwise? Was it my belief that all white people here would still have to prove themselves or be viewed with suspicion and bitterness?

The juice was so refreshing and I thought how welcome it was to be among so many black people going about their lives.

And the more I felt free to bask in the multi-racial feeling of my new surroundings, the more Trump's anti-immigrant stance seemed vicious.

But tourists are condemned to fleeting feelings and anecdotes, and I could not indulge my Pollyanna views for that long. Economic inequities in South Africa were still very present. Since the end of apartheid, access of poor South Africans to electricity, toilets, clean water, garbage removal and basic housing have all increased. But, as of 2017, overall control of national wealth was still entirely skewed, with the top 10 % of the population owning 90% of the nation's wealth, that top tier still mostly white, though now including a wealthy black elite. Poor blacks, on the other hand, remained well outside the circle of economic benefits, with the official unemployment rate at 30%.

As we made our way back to the flat, we passed a parked oversize white SUV with all blacked-out windows, except for the two windows on the passenger's side that had been smashed to bits. Countless glass shards were scattered over the grass like Christmas tinsel, the window frames picked clean down to the rubber strips.

"A break-in," said the owner of the car who had just arrived at the scene, a black woman with immediate recognition of the facts. She called the police—the robbery must have just happened while we were enjoying the promenade where she had, apparently, also been strolling with friends.

Broken glass seemed to have become a reference for the day. Later I watched from our terrace as a black man sat on the sidewalk in a thin band of shade, holding a green plastic bag full of empty beer and other bottles he had collected. He was sweaty and dazed, and he was rolling the bottles one by one down the curbstone so that a car would drive over them, I assume, and maybe the driver would get a flat tire later, wondering when or how, and the driver would suffer, not ceaselessly in the heat as the man on the sidewalk suffered, but more because the act was so random the driver would be shocked and hurt. The bottles tinkled almost musically as they rolled gently to the street. It seemed so vicious a mischief and yet, yet … why should the man on the sidewalk calibrate his revenge. His tools were the bottles, so he let them roll. Rolihlahla.

Chapter 6

The Contours of Hope

Most visitors to South Africa head to the legendary game lodges to try to spot what are called the 'big five' in the wild—lion, white rhino, leopard, Cape buffalo and African elephants. But I was too late to book even one or two nights. Plus, I reasoned, losing myself in primeval mammal magnificence was not the purpose of this trip. This trip was for me to escape my fears and, I told myself, plan my path of meaningful political resistance. This trip was about people and how could we survive in an age of reign without reason.

I thought I could find some light in South Africa's story of the rebirth of freedom won by the pure strength of human conviction and the repudiation of morbid power. South Africa's was a politics of place and time.

At Cape Town, it was almost the end of the year, almost the end of Africa—I was finishing the month with the land.

We did go swimming in the South Atlantic Ocean, limpid, calm and freezing to me, among kelp tubes the deep green color of garden serpents, floating and moving enough to seem free yet held fast by their suckers and roots, a transparent bay that gradually sloped from shallow to deep as my toes sank into perfectly smooth sand. A cleansing, and my first swim in the seas of Africa, this amazingly large continent that most Western white people still generally see as only one color—black—and only one shade of black, blurring the diversity of nations and peoples that make up the cradle of human civilizations and endow its modern greatness.

The sea to me is the ultimate thinking place, and until the chill got the best of my bones, I drifted around deliriously, so far from home, yet its worries kept me tethered like the kelp beds.

Alison drove us down to Noordhoek that night for dinner, a panoramic drive hugging narrow curves with mountains and sea on the grandest scale all around. But the land was rumbling as much as world politics, and rocks had been breaking loose. Massive mesh wires had been installed to hold the hills back and on a road normally free to use, we had to pay a toll to offset the cost of keeping the road from falling into itself.

The sun remained bright until late into the evening, and then the sun dropped away in a flight as pink as flamingo wings.

What day was it, I wondered, how long have I been here? In this hemisphere at the end of land, was it also the end of keeping track?

But why not think of Africa as where earth's land begins, and that to speak of Africa requires Africa's account first, not as ending but as prelude and introduction.

The next morning we had some errands to do and we split up, Alison to hers and me to mine, hers domestic, mine touristic.

Malls are the same the world over, sadly. I was on the hunt for some skin cream I imagined would be made with herbs and oils from African plants or berries, but that was not easy to find. Instead, all I could locate were skin cream shops that were all too proud to tell me they were selling goods from America. Their wares had nothing to do with South Africa.

Not so in the bookshop, where the shelves were packed with South African writings. I picked up Zakes Mda's, *The Madonna of Excelsior*, and was so tempted to just go on buying.

I walked around some more, then had that pleasure of spotting a bench just when you wish you would find one and took in the day-to-day before my eyes. I watched a lady dressed in starched paisley reach behind her back to hide that she was crushing a crispy roll so she could feed the crumbs to the pigeons—against the rules. These pigeons were doing far better than those Soho birds left with no pickings on Christmas Eve.

And, coincidentally, I had just learned from a bit in the *New York Times* Science section that pigeons are expert at discerning objects, all the better to tell stones from crumbs, raisins from gravel, grapes from pearls and other rock-hard baubles and sparkles that might be lying around in a rich man's place.

I was pecking around too, searching to grasp the gift of color in the sky and the land, the windblown trees, the parade of voluptuous clouds, the way to what it means to find a new continent's display, knowing it resembles other places, in fact, but is now and always its own.

Outside the bookshop café, I at last saw a mall item I had never seen elsewhere. High chairs for babies, made of rounded red-grained wood, beautiful and logical. And what were euphemistically but proudly called 'township guitars' made from flattened out Coca-Cola and other aluminum cans. A genial fellow was selling them and they had a soft twangy tone.

We had a few more domestic tasks, and headed off to Woolworth's to buy groceries. Alison would not let me help with the shopping, so I stood around at the doorway. All of a sudden, I heard the raging voice of a burly white man complaining to all the ladies, mostly white, who were seated in the café area that his bag had been stolen "while I was just sitting here having a sandwich." They nodded tsk, tsk, and he continued shouting until a customer service manager appeared. She was black, he was white, and so there it was, the old stand-off. He kept yelling that his phone and all his cards and money were in that bag. "Do you know what that means?" he pressed. "I'm paralyzed. You have to find it. What about your surveillance camera?"

The customer service agent held her ground and did her best to calm him. "We will look at that film but it's possible that a full view of the scene and the perpetrator had been blocked out by the Christmas tree," she said.

Of course, that only enraged him further, and, or was it me, was he biting his tongue against some racist comment he was about to spit out?

For sure his Christmas would not be merry until he found that bag.

We went home.

From the balcony, the breaking waves were clearly visible, the line between sea and sky a fingertip away. A sailboat struggled against the wind. All those ships plying these shores once upon a time—what must the captains have thought in the heat of the afternoon, maybe lost in off-course breeze, as misplaced as yesterday's unfinished newspaper.

Next day, more glorious weather, and we headed off to the Iziko South African National Gallery and caught a formidable exhibition called *Lefa La Ntate*, meaning 'My Father's Inheritance', by the sculptor and photographer Mohan Modisakeng. The artist became his own subject in a series of self-portraits, casting himself in various roles related to digging out resources from the earth and the spirit, including as a coal miner walking to and fro on strong gray hills, as if his body itself were the coal mine, sculpted not by earth but by muscle.

We walked and talked and stopped for lunch at the Dutch East Indian Company garden, overflowing with curvaceous tropical plants and neat rows of flowers and herbs and holidaymakers wandering in and out. It was all so mellow, compared to the ceaseless push for trade and treasure that had brought the Europeans to Africa in first place, high on the possibilities of such a vast expanse loaded with natural resources including gold, called 'colonialism' then and 'global trade' now.

Still here, a page had turned, multi-racial families took selfies and wandered through the gardens, history at rest.

Such is the freedom of travel, to suspend the memory for a time, breathe in the perfumes of another place, scan and interpret, float the mind to true or false. If all can be true, then what indeed is fake news?

Soon enough the week had passed and New Year's Eve was at hand. Alison had made excellent plans for the celebration and we were due to head off for a picnic dinner at the Cape Town Botanical Gardens to savor the evening and ring in the New Year with a special concert by Johnny Clegg.

Clegg, white, was raised in rural Zululand, among Zulu children, and is fluent in the Zulu language. He struts and incants across the stage a bit like Tina Turner, taking full hold of his audience, weaving in comments about fairness and justice, his songs invoking the land and people power of South Africa and the dreams of equality that had come along with the end of apartheid.

He told an unforgettable story as midnight approached, of the Zulu king, Cetewayo. During the Anglo-Zulu wars in the late 1880s, the British brutally vanquished the Zulu nation and exiled the King to the Cape colony. However, after several years of relative peace, the British allowed Cetewayo to travel to England, and he was granted an audience with Queen Victoria. According to Clegg, the Queen served the king tea and the king, unused to tea, tipped the beverage into his saucer and drank. According to Clegg, the Queen followed suit, not to embarrass her guest. And, at the audience, the king made the case for the restoration of his kingdom and the autonomy of the Zulu people, a request granted by the Queen.

I did research later on the episode to verify it. Indeed, according to the archivist at Osborne House on the Isle of Wight, where the audience took place, and notes from Queen Victoria's own journals, the meeting occurred on August 14, 1882 and lasted about 15 minutes, after which the king and his entourage of three other chieftains had lunch on the terrace "by themselves." The Queen did restore the king his kingdom, but there is no mention of their having tea. Various press at the time made fun of the king, including significant racial slurs. But I did also learn that it was quite a normal Victorian custom to pour tea into the saucer to cool it, and so it is likely the Zulu king was as up on his table manners as the Queen, though history had assumed he, the black visitor from afar, had been the one who had mishandled the tea cups.

The lawns were packed as darkness fell and we all watched our clocks. We'd brought some champagne, of course, but tried to jump the gun on having a sip. It had sprayed wildly when we uncorked it, but Alison heroically regained control of the bubbly hose just in time to leave us enough for midnight.

And then, the countdown—the marvelous ritual the same the world over, moving across the world, time zone to time zone, all people in the embrace of time. 10, 9, 8, 7 … Happy New Year.

The stage scene went a bit crazy, flickering with rainbow-colored lights and a drummed out brisk version of *Auld Lang Syne*, led by Clegg and sung by the hundreds of us, one voice, and one place. This was just what I'd wanted—a totally refreshed New Year rite, flushed with the truly new.

There was the golden hue of the flamboyant in the waning daylight gathered at the foot of mountains, only here.

African skies, of course, only here.

The Southern Cross constellation, only here.

Prickly pear cactus jam, only here.

And I was lost in my crazy scheme of launching all that was new in this uneven year, and the expedition of making it so; the need to dream of pages turning, continents rejoining, all familiar wastage left behind.

All the way here, reversing gravity, to find the bluest sky and the coldest sea. All in what had long been the other half of the world to me.

I had been seeking Africa, seeking history, but also the tomorrow of new peace and people, a new pour.

Only at New Year does it feel that everything that is happening can only happen once, but in a way that is eternal. We got home about three in the morning.

The very first day of 2017 found me rattling around after breakfast, endlessly gazing out to the sea. Trump was starting the New Year off by announcing he would be sticking with several hotel investments in Indonesia, despite the sordid record of his dubious partners. One of the most worrying aspects of Trump's ascent, I realized, was the degree to which the national debate had now become his theater, and we, the daily audience, fixated on his daily doings. But hard not to be obsessively on edge when someone so ill-equipped to lead the United States was about to take over precisely that job.

I had already sent my greeting emails to friends around the world for whom the New Year was just kicking in and was leafing through the replies, getting up and down to refresh my coffee. I knew we were planning to go down to the Cape of Good Hope at some point and that Alison wanted to avoid the major holidays because of traffic, so we had no journeys set up for New Year's Day. But, Alison, ever astute, said, "You want to go somewhere, don't you?"

Sheepishly I admitted I did, and she gave in. "Maybe the roads will be better than I think."

Off we went.

In fact, the roads were fluid most of the way, and even moved reasonably quickly as we entered the queue of Cape Point Park, just about land's end. The only delay we met was because the two park rangers taking in parking fees had only one credit card reader between them and the Wi-Fi signal was oh so weak. "Everyone sending hello's today," one of them said congenially, adding "and happy New Year."

We squeezed into a tight parking space just off the coast. A sign commanded: 'Don't feed the baboons'—hardly an invitation to picnic.

The land was windswept and ferocious, starkly gorgeous. Scores of visitors scampered up to the viewing point and even though I felt the joy of a common moment shared with strangers, all coming to the same special place drawn by its fame, I feared the majesty of the feeling would be diluted by the tourist jostling.

But then we started climbing until we could see the waves lapping the shores of Dias Beach, named for the Portuguese navigator Bartolomeu Dias who landed nearby in 1488 entirely unsure where he was, with more surging waves breaking green and clean over stones underwater out far away, as far as ripples could be seen.

We leaned over this breathtaking pose of land, the sea glassine, waves bursting everywhere. The coast was littered with rocks to confound ships of any size.

At this first sight of the actual tip of Africa, I was awed and gasped like a child—below, the incarnation of beginnings, and newness, a place of new position. I simply could not take my eyes from the sea washing over the crushing stones below.

At last, the hold broke and we climbed up to the top.

It was 12, 541 kilometers to New York; 9753 to Berlin; 9296 to Paris. 6056 to Rio; and 9661 to Singapore.

The center, the end, the beginning—the truest genre blur of all perhaps, where north and sound upend and long-distance figures melt into minor chords.

The day was cooling off. We took our leave of the Point.

The crowds had swelled while we were up above, and the scavenger baboons seemed to be proliferating, baring their very sharp and scary teeth, a few too close to our car.

We jumped inside and took another look at the land behind us, then gradually made our way back the way we came over the brush and moonscape.

I said not a word, trying to remember when I had felt as happy about a landscape, remembering of all places the island of Crete where I had once tap danced from stone to stone through brush and thyme and thorny thicket like this on the way to a hilltop called Savathiana. I saw my long-ago self in this moment, and I was elated, time again compressed.

Alison too seemed lost in thought until, after a while, she pointed out the brush-stroke red of natural pigments on stones here and there, as if painted faces. We reconnected with the present.

We took a route home along the coast and vast sandy beaches that were now being whipped by late day wind. We snaked along the ribbon until we reached Scarborough, stopping for dinner at an oddball local spot just as the sun was hitting the horizon but still throwing off white-hot glare enough to blind all cameras.

The place was a charming rustic pleasure, a refuge for hippies of all ages. At the table behind us, two women came to sit one after the other, each smoking a joint and having a glass of wine, golden in the African sun that was now turning into searing sunset. It was New Year's Day, and there was no need for the usual at-home things, like the Vienna Philharmonic playing the *Blue Danube*. Here was a new land that both conquered history and was eaten by it, living long enough to tell the tale. Day emptied into evening, giving in to the falling light.

Chapter 7

Mr Mandela's Walk

There was still so much of South Africa to see, my few remaining days would bring time for merely a speck. But, I was in very good hands and off we went with another friend of Alison's, Sandra, for an overnight trip into wine country, still in the New Year aura.

Traffic out of Cape Town was thin and within an hour we were long away from any trace of city. Blue-purple mountains took over and my romantic self again felt that hold of land's end and time's beginning.

We stopped for lunch in Wellington in a little garden café where I had Bulgarian yoghurt flavored with baby mint leaves and nuts, and listened. Water tinkled into a stone fountain, a wind chime rang ever so slightly, and languages poured around me, the true bells. There were tourists from here and there, and lilting English, but I could not deny the melody of Afrikaans, very much still spoken where we were, the language of the first white settlers and inflicted on their slaves, that had acquired a cultural role but soon became the hated language of apartheid. The mixing of white and black by definition meant mixed tongues and mixed memories. South Africa now has eleven official languages, including Sotho, Swazi, Xhosa and Zulu—infinite bridges to the future.

We stopped at the Breytenbach Center, a literary corner devoted to the work of Breyten Breytenbach, the brilliant poet, dramatist and outspoken anti-apartheid hero.

The curators had set up a peaceful Poet's Garden outside, pouring with ruby red geraniums and purple shawls of bougainvillea. Panels throughout were engraved with poems by South Africans, and we stopped by one called *Illusie* by Olga Kirsch, a Jewish South African poet who wrote in Afrikaans.

Alison started to translate but then just read a bit aloud in Afrikaans. Derived from 17th century Dutch, Afrikaans seemed familiar and unfamiliar all at once, and the sound was enough for then. But I later tracked down a translation in, of all places, Israel, done by Prof Egonne

Roth, a scholar of the work of Kirsch. Kirsch too had been active in the anti-apartheid movement but when she moved to Israel, she fell out of favor in South Africa since she was taken as a Zionist, which was incompatible with the pro-Palestinian tendencies of the post-apartheid political leaders.

Especially in the age of Trump, rather than the fickle extremes of politics, I preferred to remember Kirsch's poem:

'Illusie (uit Die Soeklig)

Soms as ek in die silwer skemering stap
met oë half-toe, want die ligte reën
prikkel my wange, dans en trippeltrap
verby my lippe en om my oë heen,
dan sak die stilte in 'n klamme vlaag
oor alles, donkergroen en silwergrys
die denne, en ek slaan my jas se kraag
hoër om my nek. Daar is iets wat eis
dat ek met eens met ligter tred moet gaan,
met tintelende ekstase in my bloed.
Dalk aan die einde van die lange laan
gaan ek jou, liefste, ylings tegemoet.'

'Illusion

Sometimes as in the silver evening light I advance,
my eyes half-closed as the light rain
stings my cheeks, drops dance and prance
along my lips my lids to stain,
silence descends in a damp gust
on all, dark green and silver grey spires
the pines, and high on my throat, I adjust
the collar of my coat. Something requires
that suddenly my gait a lightness gain
with tingling excitement throbbing through.
Perhaps at the end of the extended lane
in a hurry, my love, I shall rush into you.'

We left the garden, and I picked up a collection of Breytenbach's work for the road.

We drove on across rippling never-ending, granite brown hills—here the landscape was constantly changing texture as much as color. And always, that feeling of infinity ahead.

In about an hour or so, we reached the vineyard where we would be spending the night, a well-established spot off the road among the vines and enormous plane trees. Houses and villas were sprouting up all around the vineyard, just as all around the world where escalating land values make it far more lucrative to build luxury housing, even if it stays empty, than to devote the land to its original vocation of producing food, even wine.

But this was an enchanting pocket of South Africa, and I was there to enjoy it, obviously, so my self-conscious observations rang empty even to me.

We checked in and the two women at reception fell into a competion to give us directions to our rooms. The first woman, lighter skinned than the other, explained very clearly: "Go round that big tree, this left, then right," and though the three of us listened intently, none of us had fully taken in what she said. When we asked again for guidance, her confidence in her English fell away like a floorboard. She asked the other clerk, as round as an 'O', to give us directions in her better English, who spelled out the route again. Still, we got lost and made the wrong turn twice, twirling like ribbons around the maypole, around the wrong tree then at last the correct one.

Soon we were ensconced comfortably in a row of rooms deep into wild tropical gardens, fragrant and dense.

Then it was on to the wine-tasting area, where we sipped our way from deep dark Pinotage to rosé and gleaming chardonnay. The sommelier was a beautiful and elegant black woman whose hair was an object of art. I asked her how long it took to braid. "Two days," she said with a proud smile, "but I love to spend the time."

The clouds of the day blew in the evening, and the distance we had travelled drifted away as hours in my hands, here in Africa, trying to be new Africa, as the New Year began to fall in place. Dinner was succulent, but we all turned in early. Slight breezes played with the curtains, carrying the perfume of evening flowers opening to the air—now where was I, another room on the road, another dream?

It wasn't long before I was startled awake by rattling on the ribbed metal roofs. At first I thought it must be squirrels or rats, but it was a wildish gathering wind, shrill and eerie, until at last it broke like a wounded and exhausted spirit soldier in the night.

Morning came soon, and since this coffee-maker was as easy as pie, I made myself a cup and sat on my porch, gleeful in the ideal temperature and taking in early morning desires, as the hopping robin sought the ladybug, sprinklers sounded like twittering crickets and bird songs filled the trees like fruit.

There was green light everywhere in the garden, waiting for sun to hit the pool and the morning to truly begin. I sighed again in peace, with the perfect coffee on the porch, the quiet of alone and the endless search to bring forth the depth to remember it all.

But while I lavished in the morning among the bees and hopping birds, the staff of the farm were setting up for a wedding, rolling table tops like discs into place, hosing all the grass to wetness, even muddiness. It turned out that the proprietor's granddaughter was getting married, and the whole inn was being given over to her for the fete. I noticed all the workers were black, though, and only white guests were arriving.

"Good morning ma'am," the staff said to us as we prepared our departure—the wedding had taken over the place and we had had rooms only for one night. I hung out for a bit in the main house salon. Another wedding had apparently taken place just the day before. There were little pots of cactus here and there, extra party favors sitting left behind at the wine farm while the wedding couple was off now who knew where. I glanced through a book called *Meetings with Remarkable Trees* by Thomas Peckenham. I felt as though I was in it.

My bags were out in the driveway and soon it was time to go. The farmer had given us some peaches for the road, and I had placed one of mine on one of my bags while I fooled around with the zipper of another. Then, in a flash, I fantasized a scene:

The Peach Revolt: A slave is accused of stealing the peach of a guest who had left it out in the sun to ripen further on her suitcase about to be loaded and she swears she left it there. But the peach rolled off and the worker simply picked it up, thinking it had been discarded. The worker is whipped, but another slave is so outraged at this madness over a peach, he storms the overlord with a stick and chokes him, and all the other slaves revolt and run into the jungle so deep the dogs can never find them.

My mind reeled, here or home? Civil war or apartheid?

The proprietor saw us off, giving us directions to our next stop and telling us that we would pass the prison where Nelson Mandela spent a few days in a VIP guest house after his release from Robben Island, while the formalities of his freedom were finalized.

We planned certainly to stop, but when we did not come upon the prison, we assumed we had missed the sign. The only sign we spotted was one for an ATM machine, and since I needed cash, we pulled over.

But the machine wouldn't take my card for some reason, and so it was only then that we realized where we were—the ATM was just outside the gate of the very prison we had been looking for.

Seeing my confusion at the ATM, next thing, the prison gateway guard came up to help and reboot the machine. "Happens a lot in the heat," he said, adding "come to see where Mr Mandela walked free"?

And then it started. The prison guard got swept up in the drama of that historic day, for he had been there in 1990, along with thousands of others, watching Nelson Mandela re-enter the free world he had made.

The guard, a tawny-skinned Afrikaner, knew every bit of the story. In fact, he knew every inch of the monument that had been placed at the gate that we had almost whizzed right past.

"Come over here and stand on this little concrete island," he instructed me. I followed. "See, this area is in a tear drop shape to symbolize all the tears the people had to shed under apartheid."

"And all these little stones they put in to decorate it—there are so many colors because the people of South Africa are so many colors."

"And, obviously, this beautiful statue is Mr Mandela, giving a salute. What a great man. Zuma is ruining his legacy."

And there it was, out of the mouth of a prison guard, proud and sure, it seemed, a summary of recent history, the whole story in a few sentences, as he had lived it and seen it and gazed upon it every day.

And then, now deep into his memories, he asked me if I wanted to step inside the gate, turn around and "Then walk out like Mr Mandela did. Then you can see what he saw at that moment." He pointed to how far I could go and where I should turn around.

Of course, I did it, buoyed by his buoyance but feeling a little silly. But then the buoyancy won out when a young black man caught up behind me and began walking along with me toward the gate too. He had a few books under his arm and must have been teaching or working inside the prison and was just getting off. He said he had been 14 when Mandela walked out, and he had been there and walked with him. "Hundreds of us joined him when he left," the fellow recalled. "He was six hours late leaving from the time they said he would, and we were worried that they were keeping him, but then, he walked right out. What a cheer then."

And wow—how the power of his memory overflowed.

Alison, Sandra and the guard were waiting for me outside, caught up too in their own memories of those heady days. The young man who had walked with me joined them, and they, the South Africans who had lived so much, formed a semi-circle and all raised their fists like Mandela in the statue and chanted the throb of resistance.

"Amandla"—Power!

They taught me the reply: "Awethu"—Is Ours!

"Amandla. Awethu," we repeated again.

What a morning.

Chapter 8

Details of Turning the Page

The South African timeclock was ticking down and soon it would be time to leave. The weather was turning too, and wind had begun to batter the coast. Whitecaps were everywhere and I began to worry that I would get seasick if I went out to Robben Island as planned, where Mandela had served the first 18 of his 27 years in prison, in a cell the size of the back of a pick-up truck, sleeping on the floor, enduring food and water best served to goats, breaking stones in the baking sun, sentenced to life and confined to oblivion.

Plus, the interaction with the guard at the prison and my Mandela walk had begun to feel like a high point on my mission of studying resistance, and so I tried to wiggle out of the Robben Island journey. "Maybe I won't go," I said to Alison, "The sea looks a bit rough." But Alison, steeped in the years of struggle she had shared with her beloved country, wouldn't buy it.

"Everything you've been talking and thinking about here," said she, "is about out *there*." She lingered her lilt a bit on "there" and tipped her head toward that tiny rock in the ocean.

She was right.

Alison dropped me off at the ferry pier and I joined the long line of tourists who had planned to make the trip. They came from around the world, and it was just about the first time in the whole week or so that I had seen so many people other than South Africans in one place. The buzz was that of people about to visit a shrine.

Photos of Mandela were all around the waiting area—the crowd built up. Time came for boarding but the line didn't move forward.

About five minutes after our scheduled departure time, the announcement came. "The 2:45 trip to Robben Island is being cancelled due to bad weather. See the box office to rebook or get a refund."

The moan of the crowd was loud and frustrated.

Me too, since just by virtue of standing in the line and taking the time to reflect on the amazing recent days, I had myself re-committed entirely to making the trip. How could I possibly have tried to give it a miss?

Back at home, it was January 3, 2017. Trump would become President in just 17 days. The Republicans, emboldened, had opened the new Congressional session with an announcement that they planned to kill the Office of Congressional Ethics that had been set up in 2008 as an independent oversight body after corruption scandals resulted in the conviction of three members of Congress, Republican and Democratic, all of whom had spent time in jail as a result.

On the other hand, at least Trump's appointment for Secretary of Defense, James N. Mattis, a former Major General and Commander of the US Marines in Iraq, was on the record as opposing use of torture techniques. That seemed an appropriate bit of news in the face of Robben Island.

I hung around at the pier for a bit, squinting out to Robben Island as the whipping water made it harder to see. From that forsaken speck of land, the spirit of resistance of Mandela had reached the mainland, with his message of endurance, of staying alive in the name of the power of truth.

Describing his time in prison to Richard Stengel, the author who collaborated with Mandela on his biography, *Long Walk to Freedom*, Mandela said:

'I am not in a position to identify any single factor which I can say impressed me, but firstly there was the policy of the government which was ruthless and very brutal and you have to go to jail to discover what the real policy of a government is ... behind bars ... And you found, you know, the resistance, the ability of the human spirit to fight injustice wherever he is ... There were many men who could take a ... militant stand ... who would prefer punishment, even assault, rather than to give in ... In the section in which we were, you had people who were literate, widely read, travelled overseas, and it was a pleasure to speak to them ... When you sat down and had a discussion with them, you felt you had learned a lot.'

Mandela had even earlier boiled it all down in a note he wrote on a desk calendar he had somehow kept in prison, on June 2, 1979: *'the purpose of freedom is to create it for others.'*

And me? All I had to offer freedom that day was my meager try to avoid a 45-minute boat journey to the very monument of resistance, when I had told myself that coming to South Africa now was about trying to come to terms with what resistance path would make sense once I got home.

I had quipped to friends after Trump's election that I thought sooner or later we would find ourselves in jail, protesting some final insult or civic transgression by the new President. I had never had the courage to actually sit-in during protests of the Vietnam War, joining the others who got carried off by the police to jail, but I was sure Trump's time in office could come to that.

And yet, here, I had caved at the thought of being seasick.

Outside the ferry slip, a singing group called the Bonwisi Brothers held an audience rapt, the throb of The Mountain seeming to ring from their chests. I sat down and listened to regain my bearings and commitment and to think more about the courage I was going to need.

When my last South African day did come, we took a walk around the beach area in glorious morning sun.

I took a last dip in the coldest sea I've ever known, that bone-deep chill that then turns into an exhilarating swish of relief, as if the body was immediately snapping back to a new setting, like the mind in a new year.

Since the end of apartheid, all the beaches in South Africa are open to all and as I put my shoes back on, a little black girl tossed her pail and shovel onto the sand and rushed into the waves under the watchful eye of her father. I watched her face the chill and then rush out, laughing in delight at her conquest.

Above, a cloud took the shape of Table Mountain itself—flat with cirrus wisps headed out to sea, moving only slowly.

Before our last lunch together, Alison dropped me off at the District 6 Museum. District 6 of Cape Town had been established in 1867 as a 'mixed community of freed slaves, merchants, artists, landowners and migrants', according to the museum, and earlier in my visit, Alison had gotten us tickets to a popular revue based on the District's history, called *Kanala*, my first time hearing of the place.

Even as racism had been tightening, District 6 had remained an extraordinarily mixed racial area, where blacks and whites and coloreds and Sikhs and Hindus had lived together, driving the apartheid police mad. Music had been a nearly unbreakable social glue, as the people of District 6 used music at times even to code anti-apartheid messages, keeping up with US jazz and rock 'n' roll and giving it all the spice of South African flair. But in 1982, the police took to bullhorns and bulldozers and razed

District 6 out from under the feet of the inhabitants. Such a racially mixed arena simply could not stand.

And now, the museum told its story, the official permanent record, housed in the former Methodist Mission Church.

The timeline again was vividly restated. The Boer War had left the taste of venom in the mouths of the Afrikaaners who'd been slaughtered and beaten by the British, in turn feeding their hate and anger against blacks, and so as fascism and neo-fascism took root in Europe its South African version and remnants took shape as apartheid.

The museum explained how even disease patterns were used to divide people even long before, going back to the bubonic plague epidemic in Cape Town in 1901, used as a pretext for moving blacks out of mixed neighborhoods and laying the lines and boundaries for future racial segregation. Then more of the same with an outbreak of Spanish influenza in 1918. Opposition voices were crushed—the Industrial and Commercial Workers Union (also known as the I See You) disintegrated in 1920, said to have failed because of 'internal disputes', according to the police.

And, everywhere, the theme of music. There were high stacks of records by a group called The Flames, an African version of the American crooners, The Mills Brothers.

Vincent Kolbe, a well-known South African jazz pianist, activist and champion of libraries as key institutions where people could resist the limits on education imposed on non-whites, gave an interview in 1998 that had been archived in the museum:

'When the regime started passing laws like no mixed dancing, no mixed dining, no mixed playing and no mixed bands, how the hell do you run a jazz club? So that made it impossible for the culture, for the art to flourish.'

Without the thread of music, District 6 was even more vulnerable when the razing came.

Meanwhile, back to the present. There were large sheets hung as posters in the museum atrium, where visitors from near and far had signed their names and written messages. I noticed a lot of graffiti references to Black Lives Matter, the movement then coalescing in the United States to protest the ongoing street shootings of young black men by American police, for little or no apparent reason. 'There but for the Grace of God go I', a visitor had signed on a banner that hung across from the display of maps of the now redrawn District 6 areas.

I eavesdropped on a tour given by the docent par excellence, Ruth, herself black and light-skinned, perhaps once identified as a 'Cape-coloured'.

She knew the history of District 6 by heart and offered plenty of details, including reciting all the variations among the hated identity cards.

"You could never be without that card," she told her audience. "Those cards were the key to divide and rule. And it was a 90-day fine if you got caught without that card. If you couldn't pay the fine, you stayed in jail. That's the way they tried to break us down. But those cards were ridiculous. Everyone in South Africa is as mixed like a fridge cake—there were so many colors they could never have enough kinds of cards." The audience around her laughed nervously. She held them rapt.

We spent the last hours of my visit in the bountiful gardens of the Mt. Nelson Hotel, a once old-guard bastion, just steps from District 6 Museum, next door to Parliament, now with a statue of Mandela inside the gates, while Botha of the Boer War remained outside.

I watched a lean white man swim perfect laps in the hotel pool while a mallard sat on the surface nearby, unmoving. A few white tourists were sunning themselves, and I could easily imagine a black person wondering: "Why do white people want to make themselves black while they have spent so much time not liking us who are already black?"

And yet, back at home, there was very little recently to preach about, as Black Lives matter attests. Young black men were still fearful of being pulled out of their cars in America just for being black: Michael Brown, unarmed, shot in Ferguson, Missouri in 2014, on a residential street by a policeman who was, two years later, not indicted; Trayvon Martin shot dead in 2012 by a self-proclaimed vigilante who suspected him of burglary for walking in an all-white suburb for wearing a hoodie on the way home from a store to the house of friends; Philandro Castile, a respected worker in a local school, shot to death in his own car in front of his girlfriend and her child while reaching for his driving license because the white policeman thought he was reaching for a gun. In 2016 alone, 250 deaths of black people at the hands of police, according to the Washington Post, 34% of whom were young black men, highly disproportionate to the American population overall.

South Africa had come so far and so much further than apartheid, with lingering divisions and injustice yes, but the beacon through the turmoil, the Constitution, says: 'We, the people of South Africa, believe that South

Africa belongs to all who live in it, united in our diversity.' The arduous long-carried struggle for basic justice had been won.

And so I tasted the new South Africa, the unique pull of its place on earth, the poetry of its great poets and the poetry of its streets. Only a taste, however, and shortly after I left the streets of South Africa would again rock with upheaval as thousands of South Africans continued to protest Zuma, the leader who had so lost his original leadership path.

Place had been reversed for me, preconceptions upended and the new sheet of the year written on with the word 'Rolihlahla'.

Alison dropped me at the airport just about at the same spot where she had picked me up only 9 days before. The farewell made me sad—the gift of her time had been so generous. This had not been just a visit—the trip had, as I'd hoped, truly reset my clocks.

But could I do something with this fortification, this learning, this perspective? Apartheid had been generations in the making and the announcement it was over came so fast, when I had coughed in the Apartheid Museum, I had missed the key words. Decades of misery compressed into a sentence.

I thought back to Ruth and the fridge cake.

"Everyone is everything—that's what we try to remember," she had said.

Trump's election too had been decades in the making, as belief in government declined, jobs contracted, and fear of 'the other' took hold, exacerbated by racist-mongering. Racism in American never gave President Barack Obama, the first black President of the United States, breathing room or a chance to be what he had hoped for—a post-racial President. And just mid-way into Obama's first term, long-standing Senator Mitch McConnell, Republican of Kentucky and then about to become Majority Leader of the Senate, who ought to have been ashamed, dared to declare to allies gathered at the right-wing Heritage Foundation in Washington, D. C.: "Our top political priority over the next two years should be to deny President Obama a second term."

I had been in Chicago the night of Obama's historic election, at a celebration party with friends, and most of us had known Obama personally from his various civic roles. The city was electric with pride and on Inauguration Day, so was the nation.

And yet, eight years later, that same nation was about to swear into office a man as far from being equipped to be President as the raging hot sun is far from stock cold Jupiter. 'Drain the swamp,' had been Trump's exhortation, along with 'lock her up' for Hillary Clinton and 'you can grab them by the pussy' for women overall.

One insult after another, one error of fact after another, including the lie that started off Trump's emergence, that Obama had not been born in the US and therefore had been ineligible for the Presidency and yet—yet, Trump had picked up enough states to win by that electoral college landslide in states where, if the systems of the nation had been working equitably for most if not all people fairly, he would not have had a chance.

In America, we had played fast and loose with our democracy, because we have so much taken it for granted.

The people of South Africa had bled and suffered with pride, hope and forbearance. They won. They beat the curse of apartheid and wrote that Constitution.

South Africa came to rest on firm footing, having overcome so much division and looking it in the eye.

I was not at all sure my own nation could do the same.

Chapter 9

The Kathu Pan Axe

Just one night's sleep later I was back in London, ready for the next wave rides of January, at my hotel. I had left a bag of winter clothes in London while I was in the southern summer and was soon rooting around in woolen sweaters like waiting friends I was glad to see—how fast we change our focus. I looked at my pocket map of the world—all that distance, all behind me and yet now within me too.

The holiday season was now firmly ended but back home and far from the holiday spirit, Mr Trump seemed to have nothing better to do than to heap a Twitter insult on Meryl Streep, surely one of the world's most beloved and accomplished actresses, over a few words of criticism she had uttered about him at the Golden Globe Awards. The President's already thin skin was getting thinner and what an absurd use of a President's time.

I looked around to see if any Meryl Streep movies were playing in London, but none were—so for the moment I had to shelve this tiny gesture of solidarity.

But then I spotted an ad in the same magazine: British Museum, 'The Art of South Africa'.

I had only that day left to see it, given my schedule.

I glanced at my watch and looked at the Tube map. Ten minutes from Soho to Bloomsbury maximum, giving me at least two hours for the exhibition.

Down into the Piccadilly Line; deep, deeper, deepest into the bomb shelter where Londoners had taken refuge while Nazi bombers blitzed the city above and where the Holborn-Aldwych branch of track had been closed off and converted to an underground vault to keep safe some of the treasures of the very same museum to which I was now headed in a sprint.

I had noticed that the steps in most London Tube stations had shiny brass treads embossed with the name AATI, and when I had seen that same name also on the treads of the staircase down to the restrooms at the wonderful Colbert restaurant on Sloane Square, I made a mental note to look into the company one day. Eventually I did—AATI advertises itself as the leading UK manufacturer of 'cast metal anti-slip stair nosings, treads and associated products', all designed and manufactured in the UK.

No slippage of the feet thanks to the AATI treads, and so I felt free to skip down the steps of the Tube, trying to get to the museum even more quickly. The coincidence was too good to be true that a show of South African art was open for the last day of viewing on the very day I got back to London.

The show, like the museum in Johannesburg, began with cave paintings done by the earliest humans to settle the region that eventually became the Republic of South Africa, and visitors grouped up there. I zipped around the bottleneck to the next room. A single case of objects had no one studying it—I headed there and straight into a remarkable sight, the Kathu Pan hand axe. I blinked and read the card again—the piece was said to be one million years old. It was tiny, gleaming and exquisite.

The axe, on loan from the McGregor Museum in Kimberly, was too thin for practical use, so it must have been decorative, explained the curatorial card. What had I ever seen that is older? Not a single thing.

Time again, so much time embodied in this jewel of banded ironstone possibly the product of what archaeologists called 'neuroaesthetics', the drive of the human brain to create items that give aesthetic pleasure. All the days I'd spent in South Africa collected here in this object encompassing all of human history too, carved by an anonymous ancient *homo erectus sensu lato,* hundreds of years before *homo sapiens* appeared. Yet the artist was inclined to carve terraced, perfectly symmetrical forms so the axe point resembled a cluster of fossilized limpets and minuscule clam shells. But this was the work of a human eye and hand—whose, how, a million years?

And 30 minutes on the Tube to get here. Time makes us ridiculous, I was beginning to feel.

The last few days came rushing back, but relived through the various eyes of artists, room to room. On an early map displayed in the gallery here, the Dutch had called South Africa Terra Nulhus, but all that was null was their own understanding. There was work by the artist Penny Siopis of the roiling, flowing tattooed backs of black women. A landscape by Jacob Pierneef, who did not stand against apartheid, but painted trees in the veldt, reddish, seeming like the very land we had driven through en route to the vineyard. Artists Helen Sibidi and Mary Sibande dressed women in

Victorian garments, each figure as beautiful as the wine taster who had spent two days braiding her hair.

There was the bite of the police in Sam Nhlegethune's portrait of Steve Biko, the assassinated anti-apartheid hero, and David Goldblatt's photo called *Going Home on the Bus*, of the nobility of black men however separately they were forced to ride.

And how culminating to then come upon the 1994 Presidential ballot, with Nelson Mandela's photo. Mandela's face was at the top of the ballot with 18 other candidates. I had naively thought Nelson Mandela had essentially become President by acclamation, but there had been, indeed, a precious electoral process. And even if Mandela has been a shoo-in, black South Africans had a full slate to choose from, their first legal vote for President.

And thinking of resistance, here were powerful documentary photos, a museum quality scrapbook of anti-apartheid actions undertaken around the world, including massive protests in London.

I got fixated for a time on a piece by Willie Bester with a guitar embedded in cups of tin and wood, art made with day-to-day material, another version of the Township guitar I had seen.

But what truly captivated me was a self-portrait by Lionel Davis, with a map of District 6 drawn onto his head. In a flash I was back in Cape Town and the museum, in thrall to Ruth, the docent and her penetrating views. I felt one with the story—fridge cake indeed.

I was overflowing with vivid recall and walked out of the exhibition backward to take one more look at the tiny banded steel triangle from Kathu Pan, surely one of the most astonishing objects I had ever seen and would likely never see again. I kissed it through my eyes.

The exhibition had added one more lift to the launch of the New Year and smoothed over the abruptness of my return to the north and winter and disturbing nearby realities.

I would soon be headed to Europe, still of course a geographical unit but, perhaps now, more a myth that had maybe had its moment. The British pound had fallen, whether a hard Brexit or soft was ahead, and the British were wavering between these two poles, still apparently in a daze that the New Year had not erased the referendum results as a bad dream left over from 2016.

It was as if the Leavers had swallowed an expectorant and coughed up their anger, now clear of its raw and irrational power, and that the

Remainers seemed robotically compelled to execute, even though the referendum had been non-binding. The Brexit win had come from nowhere—as candidate Trump had reveled, bragging that he felt his own win had become more likely after the Brexit vote since each had been such long shots. Ha, ha chuckled candidate Trump under his Twittery breath.

And now the Brexit cough-up hung in the air.

The Remainers had failed to see the issue from the side of the Leavers, and so, like all overly narrow and self-assured leaders, they had fallen in love with their own ideas and got lost in the fog. And rather than, for example, the millions of pounds the Leavers alleged the UK would save via Brexit, a year later the remarkable contrary truth would surface—the cost of exit dues could be as high as $100 billion. What a divorce bill, all to pull away economically from countries so geographically close.

I was off to Berlin, and the distance between London and Berlin that once shaped the fate of two World Wars was now equivalent to a breath in the body of history, especially when we think that so much of England's splendid rail infrastructure was built with the idea of making it as smooth as possible for people to travel back and forth from the UK to Europe.

Even with cutting down my usual cushion time, I got to the check-in line for my flight well ahead, though it was lucky I thought of looking up from my IPAD in time to see I was comfortably waiting to board a plane for Zagreb—on time for the wrong city does not count.

In Berlin too, smooth entry from the airport to my new hotel digs, well-equipped with no-nonsense gadgets, and all possible TV channels including a Koran-based devotional station, no CNN but not a far cry from its info-tainment.

I bumped into a station whose idea of a news item was a segment about chimps that were able to drink water through a straw, but at least it was a bit of a break from the Trump 24/7.

Berlin is austere but winning, an urban potpourri of history and memory, yet vibrant with the pulse of trends, its visual reference point the iconic Reichstag domed in crystal by the English architect, Norman Foster, to symbolize that politics must be conducted transparently, before the eyes of the people.

What I loved most about the Reichstag, which I had visited in 2008, is how proud today's Germany seems to be of the fact that the Nazis never used it. The Nazis had burned the Reichstag and left its legislative halls to rot, so their echoes did not occupy the space. The Reichstag had been truly born anew after World War II, and with the Foster addition officially opened in 1999, the building had become a most popular tourist attraction, a legislative space proclaiming to all that reason in politics can return as long as we do not forget what it was like when reason fled.

The brain tends to normalize even the most repugnant and extreme events and views, to neutralize their shock so we can go on about our lives. Of course, Trump's campaign also normalized the repugnant, as we had seen when Trump, the candidate, refused to renounce the endorsement of David Duke, a former leader of the Ku Klux Klan.

Germany and Prime Minister Angela Merkel had become the central glue of the EU, always looking back to remember and guard the lessons of history, but Berlin as a city had its eyes fixed on tomorrow. My business meetings took place in a 'We Work' hub, which housed a cluster of idea-heavy entrepreneurs who leased offices here but seemed to spend most of their time in the common areas.

There was the buzz of possibility at We Work, with its transparent walls and all snacks to meet all whims all the time, all start-ups starting what, one had to wonder.

On my first morning getting to We Work, the temperature had fallen drastically and snow was falling. In the lobby, also waiting for the elevator, was a man wearing no coat, fortified though with huge orange-colored ear phones that seemed to double as earmuffs, a neck liner in the same hot orange color rolled in the space between his actual ear lobes and the earphones that were connected by the same luminous nearly hideous orange color. In sum, I wondered: an orange-wired, orange-trimmed man listening to what en route to work to do what?

I never did find out as he disappeared into We Work.

In two days, I was back to London, another mere 1.5 hours spent to return, taking back that little bit of distance that had dictated the history of half a century, the breath back in the body, time zone reversed.

I might be swallowing four continents this trip, I realized, if I counted the UK as a continent newly unto itself, which Brexit might accomplish.

Chapter 10

Roach Terrine and Other Auspicious Foods

My next stop was Hong Kong, Asia at last.

To reach Asia, I usually fly through Helsinki, a delightful if unheralded city that marks the shortest distance from Europe to Asia. Plus, to fly Finnair is to be in the hands of utter competence. Finnair seems to be that rare airline that puts more, not fewer, well-trained experienced staff in the cabin who genuinely seem to care that you enjoy your journey. Of course, this approach probably cannot last, since well-paid seasoned workers are first under the axe as cost-cutting dominates our public sphere, though Finland, overall, does struggle to try to keep faith with its efficient and well-trained workforce that expects the restful and steady pensions they have been promised. Even as the Finnish wood industry collapsed, long established wood companies were busy inventing new kinds of eco-friendly wood products to keep the companies afloat and relevant.

Finland is firmly Old Europe, trying to keep up with the future, and still expresses that people's needs must be taken into account, seeming to know governments cannot sop up social anger like sauce with bread.

And it was surely not the fault, for example, of the most courteous Finnish cabin crew that on the plane, a man was so fixated by his video game, whacking and killing like a gladiator with his thumbs, he was unwilling to stop to help me place my coat so it would not slap him in the face.

A family took up all the space in the row behind me, parents spread out as if in their living room, the children's IPads chiming constantly like a pinball game. One could not block out this noise even with earphones, while a man in my row coughed constantly without covering his mouth.

But the flight from London was short.

Baltic night comes at 4 p.m. but the streets of Helsinki still twinkled. My taxi driver told me most people in the city keep their Christmas décor until end of January to "give some light. Otherwise winter is long."

I headed straight to the Hotel Kamp like a homing pigeon, my long-standing base in Helsinki, once a literary and political hangout for the Finnish literary and political vanguard where many a day had been spent plotting independence from Russia and giving birth to democracy in Finland.

It was Sunday night and many of my favorite restaurants were closed, except for one that had re-invented itself since my last visit as a homey Slavic bistro where the pepper mill at my place had the shape of the golden dome of a Russian Orthodox church. Finland has been independent from Russia since 1917, but much of the old city retains a Russian feel.

In Helsinki, my rituals are simple. I usually spend one night there coming or going to Asia, which means at least one excellent meal, and at least one pass through the Akateeminen Kirjakauppa, the Academy Bookshop, surely one of the world's greatest book emporia located in Stockmann's department store. The Academy was designed by Finnish modernist architect Alvar Aalto with wide aisles and polished stone balconies, a space the writer Michael Cunningham has called the most beautiful bookstore in the world. And since almost nobody but Finns speak or write in Finnish, and Finns are voracious readers of worldly material, Finland is a sophisticated market for works in English translation. The English section is a cornucopia of books I would likely never see otherwise, given the shrinkage of options in the United States, writers from Myanmar and Sri Lanka, Malaysia and Turkey, Italy, France, Germany Brazil—books seemingly from all nations, all here, at least one or two copies, waiting for readers and safe at the top of the world like the famous seed bank repository in the Arctic.

The seed bank is a hedge against nuclear war that could destroy the world's seeds forever, and this bookstore to me was a hedge against Trump and his nullification of ideas.

On this bookstore day, I bought a novel by the Finnish writer, Kari Hotakainen called *The Human Part* about a woman who sells her life story to an author for a pittance, but also, in the age of Trump, Michael Frayn's classic *The Russian Interpreter*, set in Moscow.

It was irresistible in the face of the extraordinary grotesque headlines then. The media was full of the news that President-elect Trump had received notice that the Russian KGB claimed to have compromising video of him in a hotel in Moscow with prostitutes urinating on the bed, no less.

And Trump never actually denied the story. What he said was, "Does anybody believe that story … I'm also very much of a germaphobe, by the way." To CNBC he had added, "I tell everyone to be careful [who goes there.] There are cameras all over the place and you better be careful or you'll see yourself on nightly television."

The Russians call these blackmail tactics 'kompromat'—the art of compromising the other.

What worried me most, though, was that I could well believe the Moscow hotel story.

I continued my walk. Making a complete tour of the historic Esplanade is another of my Helsinki rituals, looking up at the windows of the Kamp where democratic plots were hatched, thinking that politics is everywhere, forever, as the impact of political deeds long outlast those who do them.

The tragedy of the world refugee situation, for example, knows no real limits. Even in tolerant, generous Finland, there in the snow between the bookshop and Stockmanns, was a bended figure, prostate, begging. Cloaked in black against the pure white snow, he seemed like an exclamation mark alone on a blank sheet of paper.

Soon, it became time for Asia once more, and my taxi driver told me he was a graduate student in digital technology. I asked him what he thought about driverless cars. Said he, as he cautiously navigated the greasy slick streets, "Only a human driver will ever be able to handle winter weather."

It was nearing midnight while I waited for my flight, cowering under a blanket, chilled by a too cold room. The Trump machinery was sounding more and more maniacal. That day, the President-elect had threatened to banish the media from the White House once he was in office as they continued to be 'unfair'. A madman has the reins, I thought, and the world tries to go on.

Soothing mindfulness music poured through the grates along with the too-cool air, champagne corks kept popping at all hours, even as the body clock was chiming time to sleep and act as if night was now. And how could it be that the Finnair lounge was offering 'smoked roach terrine' among its luscious finger sandwiches?

"What is roach?" I innocently asked the accommodating waitress.

"Whitefish," said she. I told her that in English a roach is also a disgusting insect, and she flinched.

****

The theme of the movie *Titanic* rose through the grates too—another bit of the flotsam and jetsam to lodge in the late night mind of the traveler in the nothing hour.

Finally, it was time to board and lift off. Up to the top, as far as one can get from Cape Town in temperature and look and, yet, my new year began not knowing top from bottom. Now I was on to Asia, one month of travels done, across borders and languages, dismay deferred, the arms of January open. Let us see.

I'd be in the air only about nine hours to Hong Kong, but even straight-laced Finnair has given in to inflight sales, keeping us awake with offers of perfume, liquor and other discounted items that, to my mind, had no place mid-air. I felt sorry for the Finnair pilot who sounded embarrassed that he too had to flog goods, urging us not to forget Finnish chocolate, adding "our chocolate is the best in the world."

But soon enough this promo mania came to an end and sleep arrived.

One of the beauties of the northern route to Asia is tracking with the day and sun. Night is abbreviated, and the pure blue of the sky and the warmth of the proximate sun come together when you wake, making it seem like the icy air outside could not possibly be cold.

Hong Kong Airport soon loomed below, the runway so close to the sailing ships on the sea it seemed as if our mega-jet when it landed would also throw a wake.

We trickled off the plane and into the advertising barrage. A giant smile crossed my face. Another New Year! I had entirely forgotten that I'd be arriving in Asia on the eve of the Lunar New Year Spring Festival and I wondered how long I deserved to feel the thrill of a new start.

As we boarded the airport tram, a string trio played lilting violin, and all the cars were festooned with a pink floral scrim, pressed perfectly flat on the windows so not a wrinkle appeared anywhere, wishing us all a happy Chinese New Year in at least five languages.

For sure I was stretching the newness of January.

In a few minutes we were in the central arrival hall—Hong Kong brings airport smoothness to an apex. It's a zip through Immigration, and a zip to the hotel shuttle bus that arrives in a zip as well. The baggage handler handles all baggage because all passengers are treated as royalty.

All around were travelers in various stages of exhaustion and excitement. But, nearly everyone, regardless of state, was phone-transfixed. Especially in Asia, the iPhone has become an extension of the hands, arms, and eyes—all seems to be possible with it, even though we know that the phone's possibilities are only as limitless as the programing inside. There are boundaries to what a phone can do. Perhaps, I thought, that is the real goal of artificial intelligence—to forever lock up our own possibilities with what is programmed inside the phone—to fuse the container and the contained, more artificial than intelligent?

Hong Kong this time would also be only a one-night stand, and an ever-ready hotel staff had taken good note. Just as I was unpacking, I heard a swishy noise. A note was being slipped under my door: "Dear valued guest, because you are staying with us such a short time, you may not have time to visit our city. So we are giving you this short article for your leisure reading."

Attached was a description of main Hong Kong attractions plus a guide to Auspicious Foods for the New Year' that listed:

Black moss=prosperity

Dried oysters=good business

(which is music to many ears in this city)

Steamed glutinous rice cake='higher year' or 'raising oneself higher'

Braised black moss pig's trotter='getting extra, unexpected income', which is desired by business folk and those having a flutter on Chinese New Year Rice Day.

I didn't know whether I would be having a flutter on Rice Day, but I did know the difference between spending only one night in a hotel in America and one in Asia—at home, they shove the bill under your door just about the moment you enter the room as if the hotel can't wait to get you out; whereas in Asia, instead, you receive a friendly note with auspicious food suggestions and tips on how to see the city in the very short time you have.

And so for me, 2017 and the west melted into China and Chinese ways, latitude and longitude now my only measure, winter to summer to winter to summer again, and lands where it's always summer that defy what calendars would have us believe.

A Chinese friend took me out to dinner that evening at a tiny only-locals-know-it fish restaurant on a crumbling concrete fishing pier near Hong Kong airport. The meal was delicious and we sat alone on plastic chairs at water's edge, even the glaring lights of Victoria Harbour invisible. We might as well have been on an atoll in the middle of the Pacific as a few miles from perhaps the most boisterous metropolis in Asia. The waitress plopped our bottle of white wine into a red rubber pail filled with ice chips and spun the bottle around with her thumbs to cool it faster, I assumed. Take a jet, spend almost nothing; my blessings are innumerable.

Next morning, it was back to the airport for a quick business meeting at the Starbuck's near international check-in—a key meeting point used by many Hong Kong cognoscenti. In Hong Kong, a lot of human transaction occurs on this pop-up, sit-down basis.

The airport was overly air conditioned and filled with false bird sounds, perhaps to honor the age of tweets, but no doubt to ward off the pigeons that had invaded the airport drawn to the crumbs of snacks dropped by the crowds to the floor.

An airport is something to see when Chinese families are on the move for Spring Festival. Huge groups convene behind yellow flags swung back and forth by tourist guides trying to keep their charges together. And getting caught standing beyond a group can cost you time.

But observing families traveling can also have its charms. I stood in line at Immigration as a young boy climbed up on the riser so the Immigration Officer could see his whole face, keeper of his own passport, his mother casting a steady, proud eye.

I passed out of Immigration—thump, thump. Good-bye Hong Kong for now. I would pass through again in a few weeks, after spending some time in Thailand where I would visit a home for migrant children where I am a modest donor.

To such children, the Trump election means little directly but could mean everything indirectly, as migration and immigration seemed to be the targets of Trump's unrelenting disdain. Yet all around the world children are forced on the move from war, famine, abandonment, poverty, indentured servitude, kidnapping and outright slavery.

The United States has played its part in this havoc, the war in Syria and support of corrupt dictators only two of the important ways. Still, on the other hand, the United States has also remained a beacon of human rights and freedom and our Presidents, in and out of office, have tried to emphasize helping and assisting people in need. George W. Bush, for example, despite his disastrous invasion of Iraq, is highly regarded for his support of anti-AIDS campaigns; Bill Clinton for breakthroughs of all kinds, including lower costs of AIDS medications and his humanitarian efforts after tsunamis and earthquakes; Jimmy Carter for supporting democracies and bearing witness to elections.

US Presidents have all made their mark on the general idea that we have only one world and we should therefore stick together. Not Donald Trump. For him, the world is just another deal board.

This was Inauguration Day and no one I talked to about it was smiling.

I've traveled the world for decades either for work or play, always indulging or being offered unsolicited the privileges of being from the U.S., of answering "I'm an American," when asked by strangers, who then smiled with welcome, even envy. And also the privilege that goes with English being the world's lingua franca, while non-English speakers may stumble and fret that their English may be flawed. Plus the privilege that goes with the US passport that enables me to travel to many countries visa free. All on top of the privilege of my white skin that insulated me 100% from external suspicion of being poor, or a terrorist, or any of the myriad nefarious ways racism can be expressed.

As an American traveler I have been denied nothing, ever, and have bopped around in this world of privilege doing my best not to flaunt or exploit these bearings I inherited merely by accident of birth, trying to avoid all aspects of the 'ugly American' cliché, and carving my own niche. Not this time.

For the first time in so many thousands of miles on the road, this time, as a result of the election of Donald Trump, I was called upon often to explain or apologize, almost as a daily matter.

I caught some of the inaugural ceremony on screens at the airport. It was disgusting enough that Donald Trump was taking the oath of office, but then, after vacuously praising President Obama and Michelle Obama for being "magnificent" in their welcome to him and handling of the transition, the new President turned his eyes straight into the cameras and pinched out the next American vision. To a waiting world, he said, "We assembled here today are issuing a new decree to be heard in every city, in every foreign capital, and in every hall of power. From this day forward, a new vision will govern our land. From this moment on, it's going to be America First."

How to be an American abroad and defend that?

Chapter 11

Asia and Back Again

I landed in Thailand problem free, feeling like an infidel with respect to my own country. Trump's Presidency was now an indelible reality.

I fumbled through the busy telephone counter line at the airport and rented a local number and phone.

I was just about zipping it into my backpack for safekeeping when it rang—*diddley dum, dilledy dum.* No one anywhere yet had this number but, here, customer service wastes no time. The carrier was already calling to see "dear lady, if you have the ring tone you like."

Ring tones as a conversation topic on Inauguration Day—as mindless as Trump himself. I had to smile at the company's concern for my mobile phone welfare but I stayed with the standard issue glings.

According to the local newspaper, Thais are reported to be spending 90 minutes a day on their phones with 27% of the people reporting they use their phones to generate revenue. A whole national economy was growing dependent on wireless signals and the *beep-beep* certainty of satellites above.

For some weeks, I dutifully kept up with the news, half away, half home, wondering each time I topped up my phone who was really roaming, my data provider or me? Soon this first Asia chapter of the year would end, but after a short return to New York City, in a few weeks I'd be back in Asia, retracing my routes.

In the international Bangkok airport, there is a towering glazed ceramic statuary dominating the center of the departure area, depicting super-sized, ancient, thickly muscled, bare-chested Thai royal soldiers wrestling an equally gargantuan sharp-toothed serpent. The tableau seems to declare that the nation of Thailand prevails; the nation never vanquished by invaders, even though you, the traveler, are entering the global brands zone where there is no nation anymore—only the nation of stuff.

It is like threading a needle to avoid the shoppers twirling their carts in and out of Prada and the like, and so I slipped into my get-away-from-others airport mode before time to board.

The lounge here was dark and dreary, with half-eaten meals that didn't seem to go with the time of day left on plates strewn around. One forlorn gentleman was building a tower of cheap potato chips interspersed with Ritz crackers. I didn't stay long enough to know if he ate it.

We boarded at last and I was headed again to Helsinki for my Finnish layover. A monk took up a window seat in business class, his orange-saffron robes bright in the low-lit cabin. Surely, I thought, he must be on some form of discounted courtesy fare. Or is his ticket thanks to the merit-making of the millions below, otherwise known as alms for the business traveler? A major scandal involving a fraudulent monk had been evolving in Thailand during my stay—I imagined I was witness to his escape.

The plane had been nearly full when I booked, and there were no window seats, so I made do with the flight map for a while. As we took off, I could well have been streaking over places I had just left, the jet I was sitting in leaving the same vapor trails in the sky I so often saw above and wondered who was flying. Was I now traveling over myself?

Dishes were clinking all around me, lunch being served at breakfast time where we were headed to keep up with the fact that we would be flying at what might as well be the speed of sound.

Soon we had crossed the Myanmar border, and were over Naypidaw, the new Burmese capital city built from scratch far inland for paranoid fear of naval invasions, but located smack on a major tectonic fault instead. Then over places I have never seen the names of, Aizari and Rikaze, sounding like twins.

Then we changed routes it seemed from what the pilot had announced and I closed my eyes for a bit just as we flew over the dot called Cox's Bazaar.

Then nothing but the Tanklamakan Desert until Almaty, due west of us. I watched the quintessential New York film *Annie Hall*, felt alienated entirely from it, flipped through the rest of the films—none worth watching. I had hoped to listen to some Sibelius but there was none, even heading to the land of Sibelius, and began a list of to-do's for when I got home.

Soon enough, we were over Russia in between Sterlitamak and Ufa—at least I thought it was Russia—and then, for sure Russia, as we vaulted over

St Petersburg no less and into Helsinki, ten hours and 8000 kilometers behind us, the pilot relieved of pointing out any landmarks or injecting any excitement, leaving it all now to us and our digital detailed maps, pushing the earth under our wings with our flimsy, inadequate fingertips, playing at command.

I gave up the map until we landed and the real world would be there.

I made my usual rinse-the-palate one-night stop and flew the Atlantic the next morning that eight hours later had become afternoon and found me making my way to US Customs at JFK airport, through the American Airlines arrival terminal in New York City, a slam into the mediocrity we in the US must now accept as the best we can do.

Utterly absent were free luggage carts and brand-new gleaming airport accoutrements that gave you a sense you'd arrived somewhere worth arriving. At least those glitzy international airport malls lend a sense that someone, somewhere has a plan. Instead of the sturdy fixtures of a modern airport, here back home in the Emerald City gateway to America were buckled damp-wafting carpets and moving sidewalks that did not move leading to an escalator also shut down, forcing us—guests?—to trudge down the tight steps to Immigration and a US Customs hall that ought to have been labeled 'Chaos Zone'.

Hundreds of passengers were pouring into the Immigration area, while frazzled American officials shouted instructions at us to go here or there, this way or that, desperately trying to distribute the ceaseless flow of disembarking people that was flooding the few available entry clerks. The lines just kept backing up, and non-U.S. citizens were lumped in with US citizens in a vain attempt to move things along. But no loosening of the lines occurred—all this version of the melting pot achieved was to irritate the officials who were besieged by non-English speakers desperately trying to figure out how to use the passport screening kiosks.

The machines required us to do twice what should only have to be done once. The scanners took forever to read the passport and then snapped a most unflattering flat-faced photograph, and spit out the so-called entry document on a flimsy piece of paper easy to mistake for a receipt from a discount pharmacy. Who bribed whom, I thought, to install this second-rate technology?

Finally, I clutched my tacky sliver of paper and the line advanced and I stood before the Customs Officer who seemed to go through all the information again, stamp the flimsy paper once, and send me on my way—

a line to get to the machine, a line to use it, and then a line to get out of Customs and into the baggage area where bedlam reigned. All baggage from my flight had long since been pulled off the carousels by the one hassled baggage handler on duty, and was now arranged around the hall in rows, so we bedraggled passengers had to walk up and down seeking our bags as if selecting them in an auction and then drag them out, or pay $6 for a cart, to leave, finally, out into the daylight and home.

Nowhere were the smiley-faced buttons that asked us to rate the service that are common in other airports. Here, the arrival process was a humiliating mess and I had yet to give in to the idea that I had to pay to avoid these bottlenecks by submitting to an intrusive government vetting process, just to smoothly and efficiently enter my home country.

A U.S Customs Office poster offered us the name and number of the Immigration official in charge of the Arrivals Hall in case we had any comments to offer. I called the number from my taxi headed into the city, but only voicemail answered, giving me an email address to which I could write. I didn't.

I felt certain that there might be a good story at the end of the search to know how the manufacturers of those ersatz passport machines won the business of the airport, but bribery stories were getting too common.

I got to my apartment, took a hot shower, went to dinner with a friend, stayed up until my eyelids drooped and then hit my bed for a deep long sleep.

I would be home for only a few days and so caught up with bills and other tasks and those closest to me. When a next trip is in the near offing, I feel neither home nor anywhere, with the near departure hovering ahead with its 'don't forget' lists and other recipes for preparation.

This break at home seemed like mere interlude on the odyssey, but I did have an anchoring bright spot when I had a lively dinner with my sister and my nephew, who had just started community college.

He was enthusiastic about his classes and told me he was reading *Civil Disobedience* by Thoreau and, in my current state of mind, we had a lot to discuss. We talked about the US civil rights movement and why civil disobedience was needed then, and when else it had been needed, or would be needed. I said I thought it was just a matter of time before that day would come again, in the age of Trump.

But he hadn't finished the book yet and the Trump regime had just started. We'd see when the two converged.

A few weeks later, I began the journey again. I was stopping in London on the way out to Asia to give a further series of talks on environmental investment and how, despite the presumed rapaciousness of Wall Street and the mantra that greed is good, many people managing money had, instead, developed ways to guide public and private investments into projects and financial tools that did more good than bad, especially to help address climate change. I thought of calling my talks 'Science and capital: how the clouds are influencing where your money is going'.

And outside the plane on the glorious day flight to London that can erase all semblance of jet lag as you fly with the day into a normal night, clouds were indeed plenty and beautiful, great white cushion puffs and crystal blue sky until, then, that gentle *bing* that told us we were up above the clouds around 38,000 feet, cruising altitude, high enough for the video loops to begin, and the Twining's lady to take over the from the real sky to let us know that tea, now called Infusions, are "the natural way to color your day."

Brexit was still haunting London in April, and nothing had become any more certain. Mrs May, though, the Prime Minister of the UK would, in just a few days, make a catastrophic blunder, calling a snap election she thought would solidify her Conservative Party majority but that would, instead, catch her entirely off-guard as the Liberal party surged, eating into her edge and forcing her into a tenuous coalition government with the most right-wing party in Northern Ireland as a last-ditch attempt to hold onto a majority and stay in power.

But when I first got to London, Mrs May still seemed to be a steady hand, and the sight of hundreds of foreigners in London either to live, work, or just pass through projected a sense that, maybe, Brexit could still be undone.

This time I was staying in Marylebone, deciding to break routine a bit, still sticking with the newness theme—new hotel, new neighborhood. I liked the setting the minute I saw the seasoned wood and staircase but especially that immediate feeling of lift with the polite words, "Good evening, Madame."

I quickly unpacked and headed for the bar, where I had a glass of a crisp South African chardonnay in honor of the Kathu Pan axe, and an open-faced salmon sandwich by way of late night supper. I had a chat with the manager, who was working in the UK though being from Italy, and we laughed at how, no matter the place or subject at hand, Italians can find each other.

Of course, with Brexit, the looming question was how much longer this free flow of people and cultures would exist. Here, every single staff member was from another country than Britain, it seemed. What would Brexit do to them, I had to wonder.

I had a meeting in London but later in the week I connected with a French friend, Katy, who had come over from Paris on the Eurostar in less than three hours and who had the very same birthday as I did, and we planned to spend a few days celebrating and exploring as we entered our next incarnations.

We headed to the Queen's Gallery at Buckingham Palace where there was a show of self-portraits, which we thought suitably egocentric for a birthday kick-off.

We took a long walk in Green Park afterward. It was still cool but flowers and vines were bursting all over and the air was full of spring and lightness. Not so at home, where just the day before an Asian-American passenger on a United Airlines flight had been dragged bodily from a plane by security agents because he had refused to give up his seat on an overbooked flight. The video of him being pulled along, nose bleeding, had instantly gone viral. And the best United Airlines could do was try to explain that they had had to solve the over-booking problem somehow and so counted on passengers to help by giving up their seats. And the calling in of what amounted to the airport Swat Team to forcibly dislodge the passenger? Oh, said United, yes, a mistake had been made.

It sounded as though United expected that we on the outside of their business, the passengers paying for their service, should help them out with their internal business shortcomings, as if we were just one big happy family and should pitch in when inefficiencies occurred.

And, it appeared, the company was ready to bloody the nose of any passenger who resisted. Resistance again, this time passenger style.

We went on to the Saatchi and Saatchi gallery, and saw a show called *From Selfies to Self-Expression*, which was a vast wall of smart phone selfies—organized visual cacophony—another form of inside being turned out. "Warm light for better selfies," crept into my mind. I had seen that somewhere in an airport ad for smart phones recently.

The selfie wall leaked intimacy and privacy, trickle by trickle, a society of in-your-face faces, a society where internal and external meet. The world seemed increasingly destined to let it all hang out. In the age of Trump, though, it was getting harder to see any limits on the horizon to how coarse we could become.

The David Hockney retrospective was packed with visitors at the Tate Britain, one engrossing work after another. I especially could not take my eyes from his phenomenal *Grand Canyon*, pieced together as if it had begun life as a piece of cracked glass.

The Canyon of Hockney's brush looked as if the earth had split and tried to get one edge to wait for the other one to catch up, but then the earth ran out of time and the puzzle was left undone.

His *Molten Red* was the color of blood meeting art, the color of a sunset in the clean cold air when daylight does not let the night take over except as a slow rising infusing and pastel-playing pink.

I wrote a postcard of Hockney's *Colorado River* using a pen from the Hotel Kamp, connecting my own dots.

April 13 was our actual birthday, the same as Thomas Jefferson's, the venerated American statesman, which did not mean as much to Katy as it did to me. We each chose a place to visit that would be new to us. She chose the Wallace collection, filled with bric-a-brac of the ages, and where we both gazed awhile at the splendid Van Ruisdael waterfalls, their cascades seemingly alive and hissing.

Me, I chose the John Keats House in Hampstead, a tiny retreat into sublime poetry and all manner of describing love of life.

We topped off the evening with other British friends, Alan and Ann, both of whom were also born in April—Alan actually shared April 13. So, toasting the good fortunes of our April quartet, we went to off to dinner at a chock-packed restaurant humming so convivially, it almost seemed like a surprise party for us.

It had been a superb birthday, and next day we went our separate ways—turn, turn, turn.

I headed back out to Heathrow and before settling in to the boarding process made one more attempt to locate a dop kit I had left on a flight on the last trip. In view of all the marketing hype of 'so glad to have you with us … please fill out this questionnaire and let us know what you think of our service' etcetera, when I actually did make suggestions for improvement, I never heard a word from marketing again. Including when I asked them for help in locating my dop kit.

British Airways, forever cutting and squeezing its margins, had outsourced its Lost and Found, and nothing of mine was found. So be it—nothing was valuable, but after many trips I had perfected the art of the tightly packed tiny overnight absolute essentials. Just reconstruct it, I told myself, and stop wasting time trying to find the original.

And maybe that is what life is about. Losing the kit now and then and starting over?

Chapter 12

The Chinese Way of Change

My next stop would be Shanghai, back through the same London airport scene I'd crossed just a few weeks ago. But, this time, I found a new corner in the lounge deliberately to avoid sitting anywhere near where I had sat recently and to joust with my contradictions. I looked around and knew I was in danger of becoming a lounge rat, a denizen of these rarified corners that were increasingly over-the-top analogies to society—permissible, decreed, established, legislated unassailable economic segregation.

Like everyone else, I surf the waves of perks and privileges, born to none of them, as no one in the lounge had earned them either except by having spent enough time or money flying sometime or other.

There was better and best, business and first, galleries and Concorde, each a level more luxurious in theory, but all luxuries here are consumed too fast to actually be luxurious, as we are urged to buy our way into higher levels—more tea sandwiches, more priority or deference, more legroom, more perks to decline and more free goodies for those who can afford to buy them by the carload, white men lifting thin legs while dark skinned women sweep underneath saying, "don't worry sir," or "sorry, sir" as if this was a plantation house in any period of colonial history on any continent. And it seems the richer people seem to want to look, the more free stuff they seem to consume, champagne for the having, so they have it, day or night, breakfast or lunch, non-stop pouring and picking at the endless buffet.

At home, Trump had just about assembled his Cabinet, a group of ideologues only an ideologue could put together. Among them, the head of the Education department, dedicated to the privatization of public education, claiming she believed education was an investment in individuals not systems, as if one could happen without the other; an Energy secretary who, as a former Presidential candidate had called for the demise of the department he was now heading, though then he could not remember its name; a Commerce secretary, married to the Education secretary, who was a laissez faire capitalist steeped in conflict of interest, such as in continuing to hold substantial stock in shipping companies while his role required him to develop trade and shipping policies that could increase the value of his shares; a Housing and Urban Development secretary who derided public housing as a hand-out, though he himself had grown up in public housing; an administrator of the Environmental Protection Agency who was dedicated to dismantling environmental regulation and dismissed all climate change science as fabrication; a Secretary of State whose only diplomatic experience was as an oil industry executive dependent on Russian goodwill for his deals; and a Vice President who spliced his every word and public policy idea with explicit Christianity and doubtful devotion to the separation between church and state.

In Trump, they all saw a way to perhaps get even with institutions they had vilified, maybe hated, for a long time, or at least that is how they sounded in their confirmation hearings when I caught bits on TV as I moved along.

Maybe, I thought, Trump had been told that when Barack Obama assembled his Cabinet, he had referred extensively to the bestselling history, *Team of Rivals*, about Abraham Lincoln's Cabinet, and how Lincoln chose his advisors for diversity of views.

Except, in Trump's interpretation of the book, the Cabinet he chose was more like a team of scorpions, each infused with intense personal ideology, so driven to use their new post to advance their extreme views that perhaps they could never collaborate to get anything done beyond their own narrow interest agenda. Maybe, I hoped, the Trump Cabinet would never pull together. Maybe the ideology of one would nullify the ideology of all. Maybe, like scorpions, they would sting each other's backs and paralyze each other—so nothing they intended to happen could happen.

I was hardly proud of wishing for government by paralysis.

"Go to gate," said the screen. I obeyed.

The boarding area was already crowded, but a warm melody rose above the routine shuffle. An airport worker was sweeping the floor near the gate singing "darling, I am thinking of you," his hair curled up in a rainbow knitted cap wobbling on his head like an overloaded fruit bowl. He just kept sweeping and singing with an assured lithe elegance of voice and posture. I was glad to be listening to him, until the next reassuring sight—a well-turned out cabin crew, on time and looking ready for work, stepping on board just before the rest of us.

The BA plane had the same tight seats, the same flickering screens, the same Twining's lady, and all the same movies, and I felt for a bit that I had gotten stuck in a selfie video loop of my life. But, still, as much as I complain, I do still love that thrill of being in the air, especially when Shanghai is the destination.

What an intoxicating city.

Dense fog had narrowed the huge airport down to one runway, so we circled for a time, but soon enough I was speeding through the formalities and punching 'Excellent' on the Shanghai Immigration customer service survey console buttons, just below the video message welcoming us to China and explaining 'the power of smile'. Outside, there was even a V-VIP parking area.

I settled into my taxi, more than comfortable enough, and the driver handed me a cold towel and asked if I wanted music. I didn't, so we rolled along in silence at not one kilometer per hour above the speed limit, which seemed awfully slow, but soon enough I was arriving at another favorite hotel. A few years ago, I'd wondered why this hotel had a scent, and the concierge was only too pleased to tell me: "Oh yes, madame, that is our signature perfume—white tea."

That's when I learned that many hotels were using a signature fragrance to brand themselves in the minds of their guests, under the theory of Pavlov's nose, I suppose. I had to admit I liked that white tea fragrance, and here it was again, this time wafting lightly even outside as I stepped through the revolving door. Was everything repeating?

Up in my room, the attentive bellman showed me around, making a special effort to point out the 'hair driver', that indispensable item the location of which so many other hotels have turned into a game of guess where. No need here.

I pulled open the curtains. There, the Hangpu River headed to the China Sea, with ships feeding themselves one by one like floating leaves into the flow, never ceasing, just like the city.

I knew where to get the ferry across to the Bund side, costing about $1, and the boat was packed with locals out for the day, some on a corporate outing, it seemed, all wearing the same pink baseball caps.

I had not noticed that the day was Easter Sunday in the west—this seemed to be my year for traveling against all the big Christian holidays.

Here, Easter was just an ordinary Sunday, although an especially clear day. On such warm 'blue sky' days, no one who doesn't have to stay home, stays home. The whole city had stepped outside it seemed, but I knew that even the multitude swirling around me was only a fraction of the population. Shanghai had grown from an already staggering 16 million people to 23 million in just ten years, its modern growth branded by its spectacular signature buildings—the bulbous Oriental Pearl Tower and other twisting and swirling shapes seemed to have been tossed up into the air as if nothing but oil on canvas.

I had the afternoon free and strolled up and down the riverside walkway, one person among thousands. I could not get enough of that skyline. Of course, to build the river walkway, many little sundries shops had been forced out, and the price of modernizing Shanghai has been cutting away a part of its Asian heart. But the people of the city obviously loved this open space and basked in the mood of relaxation, as if Sunday was that one day of liberation from rules and prescriptions.

I ferried back to the Pudong side when night had fallen and had a quick bowl of soup and beer at a riverside restaurant under a handful of stars.

The next day I was due to give my first talk to young financial service staff, the next generation of Asian money managers. My hosts treated me with kid gloves, picking me up at the hotel and walking me to the classroom we'd be using for the talk just a few minutes away. When I had first started coming to China regularly in 2006, English was spoken by only a few senior executives, and then it was stiff and formal.

Now, English flows easily, and it is clear that the big investment China made in English education in universities has paid off. My hosts as well as the early bird students already seated in the audience peppered me with questions, including "Miss, would you like a sandwich?" since they did not want to eat without asking me too.

The classroom was high above the river, our little room lost among the shimmering skyscrapers. The neon turned the view into a wild amusement park of reflections, including a replica galleon sailing down on the river that, in the array of lights, I could not tell if I was imagining or not.

After my talk, there were more questions, and two of the students walked out with me and, no doubt to keep in touch for possible help in getting a job, asked for my card. They zeroed in on the Mandarin side very carefully, and then complimented my "lovely Chinese name", for which I can claim no credit. All credit goes to a translation service that created my bi-lingual cards, transposing my name to Mandarin characters that match my phonetic and mean roughly, I'm told, 'serious and nice'.

Back at the hotel, the eateries were too fancy and anyway I was too late for them, but not too late for the downstairs nearly all night Grill, where the music tried to rock and the beer on offer was almost all from other countries, but when I expressed disappointment not to be able to order a plain old Chinese Changdo, the all-accommodating waiter ran off to get me a bottle from upstairs somewhere.

Over the beer and a bowl of vegetable soup, I read in the *Shanghai Daily* that there had been more blue sky days lately in the city of Lanzhou, but that Qinghai Lake had turned mysteriously pink. Such are the color contrasts of air and pollution in China.

The paper also reported that a private zoo in Harpursville, New York, had raised millions of dollars by putting a video of the birth of a giraffe on YouTube. Meanwhile, too, the paper said, a manhunt was underway for an Ohio man who had committed a cold-blooded murder, filmed himself in the act, and then streamed the film on Facebook.

I left my table to find the waiter and pay the bill and it was so dark in the bar, he had to use his pocket mini-flashlight to make out the charges.

I did not want my stay in Shanghai to end and so I took a stroll on the elevated illuminated promenade that circles among the spires, a Shanghai version of New York's High Line, new since my last visit and always teeming with people. From that vantage point, the city defies its weight, the upper level at a remove from the hubbub, free of cars.

I walked another half an hour until, pop, all the lights around the walkway went off at once for the night. If the Shanghai skyline was going to sleep, I guessed I had to too. Luckily, like the bartender, I carried a tiny flashlight and fished it out to get back down to the street.

In my room, I opened the rubbery opaque night curtains and their gauzy doubles too. It was glorious to bring the river into the room even at night. Could I have been born under a raindrop, I wondered, as the river finally carried me to sleep.

In the morning, so many ships were already flowing to and fro, I still didn't want to leave the view. I decided to call room service for breakfast.

"Can you speak again the time, lady?" the in-room services clerk said when I called down. I repeated it and on the dot, room service arrived with a full table set with a rose and everything exactly as I had ordered it, the white-gloved waiter warning me too that the milk was hot. "Be careful if drinking it," he said sweetly on the way out.

In the car back out to the airport, the white-coated driver, gold thread trimming his cuffs and collar, offered me the perks of the day according to his protocol. "Water, miss?" and "Wi-Fi, lady?"

Then, as we came to a standstill on the highway, he made a comment in Mandarin, looking back at me expectantly. I smiled and tried my mumbly version of "wǒ búhuì shuō zhōngwén" meaning 'I do not speak Mandarin', and waved my hand in that so-no-point-in-speaking-to me-as-I am-a-mute-and-cannot-understand way. At that point, undaunted, he tapped some keys on his smart phone, then turned the screen to me so I could read and listen while the Chinese equivalent of Siri spoke the English words "car, bad" that were also printed on the screen. I took that to mean 'dreadful traffic,' and said "dway-yes", which I can say in Mandarin clear as a bell. He smiled and returned his eyes to the road.

Then on to China Eastern, where the boarding process was chaotically first-come, first-served. But then inside the plane, serenity reigned and the uniform-perfect hostess escorted me to my seat as if I were a princess. Go figure. China mystifies and mesmerizes, no matter where or when, though for sure it's become a selfie nation of non-stop self-immortalization.

The two other passengers in my row kept right on snapping even during our rocky landing in Dalian, my next stop. Out each window there were buildings as far as I could see, a density such that I had to wonder if we had ever actually left Shanghai. This city was officially established in the late 1880s, and its modernization started a hundred years later. Today the city seems all built up. Out on the tarmac, there were dozens of brand new machines and vehicles ready to go—gleaming trucks and ladders, pristine baggage handling carts, all forms of moveable stairways, rolled up, rolled out. The airport was loaded with inventory.

The road to the city offered no let-up in the sea of buildings, no trees in sight, but a billboard announced a coming development or retirement home perhaps called 'The Gentle Folks' where, according to the ad, flowers bloomed from the heads of the residents.

The reception staff at the hotel fell over me to be nice—"we have chosen for you sea—a beautiful room."

And it truly was, with a spectacular view of the Donhai Bridge that ran for miles and smoothly disappeared into the mist like scenery running off the wings of the stage.

Here too was an apotheosis of toilet gadgetry. Sensors ruled. The toilet seat popped up when I so much as stepped close, the toilet self-flushed and the seat popped down immediately, keeping itself warm in between.

This up-down-heat was too much, and I unplugged the system to kill the heater, but I then found there was no way to flush manually. The reception staff were so proud of their hotel I didn't have the heart to ask them to decommission their toilet, or give the slightest hint of displeasure. Come the revolution, I knew, there would be no pop-up toilets.

I gave my talk at a local university and the audience of students and faculty stood when I entered the room. Interactions with alert and inquisitive students and professionals are always rewarding, but especially in China where almost everyone in the audience seems to regard learning as the only passport to anywhere or anything—moving up the ladder in China, or leaving it.

Contacts with foreigners and foreign news are precious, still.

"Does your President Trump believe in climate change?" one student asked me, "We hear that he does not."

I replied that once the President had, but now he said he did not. "His words and actions do not match his mind," said I. I wanted to give them some hope.

"How long before they become one thing?" the young man pressed.

I had outsmarted myself trying to hedge my answer.

"Let us wish soon," I replied, "it could happen tomorrow. He likes us to guess about him every day." The student grinned.

A student escorted me back to the hotel and wished me "more good travels". Then he was off, mobile phone to his ear.

"Dalian, Dalian." This was the hotel's restaurant on the 46th floor and the receptionist, super-well trained in the ways of welcome and upselling told me I might like it. "It is so beautiful," she tempted.

So I said fine, planning to think about it, but then she pressed, mentioning that Dalian was 'hot'. At first I thought she meant I would have to dress more lightly, but what she meant was that the restaurant was so popular, I had better let her book me right away.

I had no reason not to. When I arrived upstairs, my table was ready, just what the receptionist had promised, right on the windows with a perfect view of the bridge that turns many colors while you're not looking and then seems to freeze into one color just as you do—a bridge that goes for 80 kilometers and seems to never end.

China overdoes, then just waits for people to come and behold, as they always have and always will, and sometimes when you leave, it feels like your heart should break.

I had most of the next day free and took to the streets. Dalian has a Coney Island energy, at least down by the sea, where there is an amusement park and wide open-air patios and walkways, with bronze sculptures of ice skaters crouching in high-speed action, so life-like that people pose with them for photos, trying to imitate that impeccable Olympic form.

The crowds seemed liked pastel flocks—groups organized and wearing caps and shirts all in the same colors, as if all the visitors in Dalian were divided into teams. I guessed that maybe this had been a special visitors' day, as there were dozens of long-distance coaches parked on the traffic circle—many buses, so many teams, and a nation of team-builders?

There were so many people around me moving and waving that at times I could not tell the crowd from the octopus amusement park ride just behind them twirling its countless cable arms.

I was the only foreigner in the vicinity, it seemed, and I was dying to take photos but I was a bit afraid of being trailed as a spy, which has never crossed my mind anywhere before. But this was the age of Trump and right around then he had sent ships in the wrong direction, apparently, as part of his blustering and huffing in the Pacific to intimidate Kim Jong-Un, the North Korean leader. North Korea was on high alert and, said CCTV that morning, so was China now too. I kept my camera in my pocket.

Up a hill, the Dalian Castle Hotel dominated, and I headed for it out of curiosity. It was a faux batiment outside, and inside a cross between Versailles and the Crystal Palace, a leaded glass dome over the lobby, with silver and gold satin furniture, expansive space lavished on itself. The Castle will never be downsized. It was the Trump Tower of Dalian.

I mistook the 'Y' sign in the lobby for the women's restroom, but the stylized 'Y' stood for Yuan and the ATM, which was all by itself in its own marble vestibule and encasement, so protected like a sculpture that I could not rule out it was someone's idea of a work of art. The Castle hill had been worth climbing, just to experience making that kind of mistake.

Faberge-faux Easter eggs were still to be seen here and there, sitting in baskets of flowers from last week—Easter, like Christmas, was going universal. On the other hand, at the Castle café, the local touch was on offer as 'distinguished champagne coffee in this blooming season' or, for the special tasting menu 'Zhenbao spring bamboo shoot feast'.

Electronic Mozart piano suites tinkled in the background everywhere, and only Chinese guests seemed to be milling around, of all ages and manner of dress, including astro-speed running garb, all dripping money. Intricate black wrought iron à la the sumptuous gates of Parc Monceau in Paris trimmed the mezzanine. And if in my hotel the toilet seat popped up and down to spare me lifting it what, I wondered, could be in store in the bathrooms of the Castle?

It was a long way down to nothing from here, even for China's rising middle class.

The Castle was the essence of overdone—who thought of it, I had to wonder. But then Dalian itself spoke to some form of high concept—an urban creature by the sea, an entirely new ribbon of mansioned cityscape, the people's shop window, hugging the coast with a people's amusement park at the bottom of the hill, the transient royals for a day or a week up here. Voilà. Layered living Dalian style. Modern China creating itself all at once.

This Castle was, of course, not the first lobby I had ever squatted in to take advantage of Wi-Fi, but for sure the first of this surreal opulence. China perplexes—such strong national pride and yet such emulation of the very West it feels the need to outdo. ATMs in marble—and the end of let them eat dirt.

Room rates at the Castle started at 3900 Yuan for basic deluxe, about $600 a night, to the Presidential Suite of 15,800, about $2400.

The hotel was full, the receptionist let me know, but she said she'd gladly take my email address to let me know when they expected to have rooms, not that I'd been seriously looking.

When I left my hotel next morning, now seeming sparse by comparison, so early it was still dark, the receptionist handed me a shopping bag breakfast I had not asked for—enough muffins and fruit for three persons. The western idea that more is always best was definitely taking hold in China. I could not possibly eat all of that at any time of morning, let alone dawn, and so I gave the bounty to the check-in clerk at the mercifully empty check-in line, the antithesis of yesterday's check-in long march.

And yet, even as the force of gadgets and all electronic flush the toilet tricks and doodads take over, at the airport itself local village farmers sat just outside the double automatic doors guarding large wooden baskets filled with ruby red cherries the size of ping-pong balls, ready with pre-folded cardboard boxes to fill in a jiffy so passengers could carry them on board just like any other duty free purchase, though for cherries there were no duties charged.

Chapter 13

The Crane and the Peacock

Soon I was skimming along again between airport and town, now in Beijing, the centerpiece city of this Asia trip, with a billboard proclaiming 'China Service Mansion' as a greeting, a building complex itself as large as a beginner-size Chinese city. The traffic was again 'car, bad'. The car doors snapped shut.

Even with the Chinese Siri, no driver yet speaks enough English to understand what I mean when I try to get across "please unlock the doors." They think I mean open the doors to let me out right then, so they look at me as if I am insane. But it's just that I loathe being locked into the back seat of a car like a child, or as if I was hiding from body snatchers. Plus, I also have a lack of faith in car electronics. In the event of an accident and the electronic doors took a hit, why should the car lock work any more easily than a coffee machine? And why would a smashed electronic lock unlock?

"Cabin crew, put all doors to manual," says the pilot when a plane has landed. That's what I want in a car, so the driver and I could escape in a pinch.

But in China, I simply could not communicate that paranoia, so I lived with it and took heart in the next billboard advertising the Nine Mile Fragrant Bank.

Here in Beijing, I gave a talk in a large plenary session. Again the crowd was bursting with enthusiastic questions about green finance, one could almost believe the dream could come true. China does this to me—if I give in to my magical thinking skills, no task seems too huge.

After all, I later learned on my first formal tour of the Forbidden City, that in the 15th century, to tackle the task of hauling a huge marble slab weighing 300 tons 80 kilometers from the quarry to the Emperor's palace, Chinese engineers conjured a plan to use 1000 donkeys and their herders and created an ingenious pavement of ice. The engineers, thinking a year ahead at least, ordered the massive digging of holes along the needed route.

Then, the holes were filled with water. When the water froze, the donkeys pulled the huge stone along the ice road to Beijing, safer than using wheel-driven carts that would not have held the weight. This massive stone-skidding solution was undertaken two hundred years before the first Thanksgiving dinner in America.

And yet, as I took this in, I had to wonder whether humans, especially we in America, have become bored with earth, seeking greater leaps for thrills of dubious importance. I had read that very morning about humans wanting to conceive infants in space, a real challenge presumably given the potential for all appendages to float once outside of earth's gravity, and now even Jeff Bezos, the founder of Amazon.com that had made mincemeat of retail bricks-and-mortar shops to no productive purpose as far as I was concerned, had joined the Mars bandwagon suggesting that we better begin planning to live there. Easy for him to say, I thought, after he had ruined Earth for bookstores, to say the very least.

And compared to our magnificent home planet, Mars is a lifeless nightmare, suffocated by methane rain.

Anyway, back to the crane and the peacock. Long life, royal flair—the Forbidden City hypnotizes and magnetizes, no matter how far we believe we have come, and can go. There were young hip Chinese everywhere, mobiles in hand, yet still fingering in awe the massive brass locks the Emperors had left behind.

Before Mars, I thought, so very much to still learn and do right here.

According to the Temple of Heaven, my guide said, "Heaven is round, earth is square"—that will surely keep us guessing awhile, I thought.

We went up to the 798 District in northern Beijing converted from a 1950s munitions complex and just breaking out of its shell when I first started going there, then a flashy new zone. But homogenization had found 798. Just a few years ago, a vanguard photo gallery I knew, one of the first in the area, was proud to showcase original cutting edge work. Today, actual original photography was relegated to a corner of the gallery, which had morphed into a gift shop selling mostly dispensables including a business card holder that popped cards out like the flame from a cigarette lighter—high design, high price—$100, made in Holland.

Outside, two girls who looked like models for porcelain art ware, each wearing the same long dangling wood panel earrings, kept taking selfies even as crowds almost knocked their selfie-wands and phones from their fingers.

All around, other tourists on the street were clutching bubble tea or other creamy drinks, something in the hand always, if not food or drink, the iPhone endlessly being scanned as if a cascade of text was hovering above and about to land on the screen at any moment. The street was filled with people seeking messages—I wondered what the Mandarin was for the person who never gets any.

I stepped into the Ullens Center for Contemporary Art, to see a show called *The New Normal*, where most of the work was so conceptual I desperately wished I could speak to the guards. What must they be thinking about standing watch over braided rope draped over wooden crates, or empty rooms with video screens and posters declaring 'Reality should not hold back your need to project an image' or 'Let smog removal give you back your blue sky!'

Whatever happened to guarding jade Buddhas, perhaps they were wondering.

But the exhibition was busy with visitors from everywhere, including many Chinese. I wondered about us all—where was the line between curiosity, boredom and true exploration.

According to the exhibition description, the show took a 'destabilizing world as its point of departure. 'State of Exception' refers to a situation in which established laws and regulations are abruptly suspended, replaced by temporary conditions that in turn become the status quo. China's new role as a champion of globalization amidst a worldwide populist backlash is among the most unexpected of these reversals. Artists have been invited to reflect on these uncertainties in a fragile and unpredictable present.'

Perhaps we could invite the same artists to reflect on America's new 'State of Exception', I thought.

I asked my guide if he thought that tourism would be in the end the main force changing China. He answered simply, "Don't forget, Marco Polo was a tourist. He got in even after the Great Wall was started."

At the end of the exhibition was a public space where visitors could talk further about what they had seen and a group of Chinese students seemed involved in an animated conversation with a museum official. On one wall in this public area, various books has been put on display and labeled essential reading of our age. Among them, either in translation or original language: John Berger's classic *Ways of Seeing*; a book of conversations between Umberto Eco and Jean-Claude Carrière; studies of Le Corbusier; and the recent American best seller, *Genius*, about editor Max Perkins.

We went on to the Three Shadows, a less commercialized photography space and daring still. An exhibition of the Galactic Reading Group proclaimed: 'Nobody reads but silence sounds.'

I moved on to the next room and watched a video produced by the Relatives Searching Volunteers Association about women who had been raised outside of China who had returned to China to search for their original birth parents. Roughly 120,000 Chinese children were adopted abroad from the mid-1990s to mid-2000s, many of whom were girls, due to the One Child policy and the once strong cultural preference for boys. Women that gave birth to a girl were often bereft and families faced a huge fine if they had a second child, so they had to somehow dispense with the first.

In one heart-rending sequence, when a woman who had returned to China was at last re-united with her original family, including siblings she had not known she had, she burst into tears of gratitude, but her relatives made light of her emotions.

"It's no big deal now, right?" said a half-sister. "It all worked out for you." The lost girl was even more distraught.

In another sequence, one elderly woman sent word through her neighbor to her long-lost daughter who was waiting outside that the mother could not come to meet her "because after I abandoned you on the street I sank into the quicksand of sin."

Recovering time defies us, despite gargantuan efforts.

That evening I was due to meet a colleague for dinner and I wandered around Beijing's hutong area, also now both refurbished for western comfort and forever changed. All tableaux here were mixed. I watched an elderly Chinese couple perched across from each other on a children's swing set, eyeing each other lovingly and then looking down to check their phones, then up at each other again, utterly carefree as they see-sawed back and forth.

I had been charged with choosing the restaurant for the evening, and so I did some tourist reconnaissance. Here are some dishes at a restaurant where we did not eat:

Sweet juice explodes the shrimp
Blood flushing frog

The area around Houhai Lake was packed with tourists on this warm and pleasant Saturday night, and restaurant space was scarce. But finally we spotted a tiny storefront diner where the proprietress waved us in and served us delicious basic crispy chicken and vegetables.

My colleague, Sareh, is Iranian and so we talked a lot about the tensions between Iran and the United States, senseless to us both. She thought Trump and the former President of Iran, Mahmoud Ahmadinejad, were cut from the same cloth of fantasy bluster and unpredictability. Trump's doings were becoming a universal reference point.

He had just that day announced a tax cut 'bigger than any tax cut ever' without a shred of detail and to the apparent surprise of his close financial advisors, including the Secretary of the Treasury. Meanwhile, he was reportedly consulting roughly once a week with a bevy of amateurs, including friends and outsiders and self-appointed advisors, who often second guessed the White House staff and Cabinet, keeping the circle spinning.

We said our goodbyes and I decided to get a cab to my hotel later and first walk a bit through a long narrow park that I used to thread daily on my earlier trips to Beijing. But I was much further up the avenue than I realized and much farther away from the corner where I thought there would be plenty of taxis. As I walked, that corner was only gradually getting closer, but what a joy to be out on this street on this balmy busy weekend.

Two couples had set up a boom box that played ballroom music and were whirling in each other's arms in circles on the sidewalk. Up and down the street, others Beijingers walked their dogs, some chatting to their pets like they had been long lost. There were many fancy hefty Labradors, large pets and large cars the proliferating toys of newfound disposable income.

When I finally reached the corner of Chang An Avenue, there were no free cabs in sight. But the driver of a motorized three-wheel rickshaw had spotted me and wheeled around to my side. "Bargain," a little voice told me, "that's what people do." But I hate bargaining, and so I do it half-heartedly or at the wrong time. Like then. The driver asked 100 yuan for the trip to my hotel, but when I offered only 80, he sped off. How dumb, I thought. You are tired and you want to get home and you just saved yourself $2.50. But the entrepreneurial driver knew his trade and gave me just enough time to reconsider my folly. Then, zip, he doubled back to my side. I gave in to the 100 and we went careening down Chang An into six lanes of auto traffic all around, his tiny vehicle like a beach chair on the boulevard.

But then he made a sharp turn, and we zigged and zagged through a maze of narrow lanes, lone on the move. I was being tossed around in the back seat like a peach pit in a basket and thought the backstreet scene was perfect for a shakedown. But the driver kept up his speed, and when the dark road opened out onto a police station, the driver circled around it effortlessly in full view of the cops standing outside, so I concluded he had no criminal intent. Whoosh. After conquering the labyrinth and avoiding more 'car, bad', we got back onto Chang An, beach chair rattling, whizzed through an underpass and emerged right on my corner.

And just in time for me to catch what was up outside Restaurant 26, an inviting café across from my hotel that I had not yet had the time to try. I heard heavy metal clangs and looked over to see a dozen waiters, all in white jackets, rolling a giant heavy stove down the stairs of the restaurant, a step at a time, to more or less bounce it onto the sidewalk. *Bang, bang, bang.* When the stove was safely settled on all fours, the waiter team picked it up in unison, chanting a rhythm in Chinese—"1-2-3 all lift!"—I assumed, and they inched it along that way as a group, picking it up, putting it down, and giving themselves a pep talk each time they had to rest.

They lifted and walked the stove slowly around the corner and then up some more steps into what seemed like a side door to the same restaurant. All this effort may be because they could not move the stove through the restaurant itself, surely because they seemed to have taken it out one door and into another.

Anyway the stove haul parade seemed as miraculous as the Forbidden City marble being slid along on the ice. Team-building by a nation of team-builders. Trump, on the other hand, was constantly ridiculing others, even muscleman movie star and former governor of California, Arnold Schwarzenegger, for having lower audience ratings than Trump supposedly garnered on his former reality TV show and political springboard *The Apprentice.*

The next day I was again in need of a cab, and this time finding one was easy. I was returning to my hotel after a meeting and had been closer to my destination than I'd realized. The fare was only 20 Yuan. So when I offered a 100 note to the driver, he pulled out 80Y in 20Y notes and said in English, "Okay you give me hundred I give you 80."

But when I handed him the 100, he rejected it furiously, shouting "Beijing 100, Beijing 100!" I tried another bill. He held it up to the light and took it.

I remembered that at the Ullens Center too, they had also rejected one of my bills after they ran it through a sorter, presumably to spot counterfeits. But all my Yuan had come from ATMs in China, including the marble magnificent at the Dalian Castle.

The next morning was again time to take on the airport. I flipped on the TV while I was packing and watched an ad promoting a 'Disruptors Fund', a Fin-IT fund based in Singapore, thinking it might present some interesting projects. But mostly it promoted investments in augmented reality, showing subscribers watching inter-galactic warfare while working out at the gym, as if the goal of IT innovation is to put a show inside your eyes you'd never buy an actual ticket to see.

Curiosity, exploration, boredom? The same dice rolling.

I flipped to CNN and then suddenly the screen went black while I was watching a news clip of a woman confronting a tank during protests in Venezuela. The video zapped off just when her image appeared. Immediately I thought of Tiananmen Square and indeed when the image reappeared, the CNN commentator called it a "Tiananmen moment" but somehow his audio got through while the pictures did not, as if censors see before hearing, or maybe the translator had taken a tea break.

Still, truth, like water, can slip through cracks.

It was time to leave and I called downstairs to ask for help with my bag. "Take a rest" is the way the Chinese have learned to say "wait a minute."

We again took up the airport road. According to Price Waterhouse Coopers, China will become the world's biggest economy by 2030—some say much earlier—and it keeps building huge buildings and offices that surely must be empty most of the time. Trillions in dollars and resources of glass, wood, energy and cement are locked up in structures that may never return their value.

But still builders build and many are kept employed. The Dalian Castle is a rarity but bubble tea for the masses is not.

The US appetite for cheap goods surely helped fuel China's economic burst, and Walmart and China may have been the most symbiotic commercial relationship in world history, on par of Marco Polo, as the expanding Walmart chain provided China with shop windows all around America. The insatiable American drive to consume cheap products became complicit in the outsourcing of jobs to China to make those products, and so, among other factors, the waning of American economic well-being. No developed nation's manufacturing base could compete with the low wages of China for a time.

That tide may be turning, as Chinese living standards rise and wages too, but that day Donald Trump had called for trade embargo of China if China's 'unfair' practices did not end.

He plays the wounded with China, and foreshadows trade war, but the Chinese will just wait him out.

At Beijing airport, a scent of oranges led me to a machine that presses fresh orange juice just across from the ladies' room, but I skipped it. I was en route to Seoul and simply settled down near my gate in what I have come to call the 'ZC Zone', for Zero Contact, that rare zone in time, usually at an airport, where there is no one to call who needs to be called, and no one knows how to reach you or where, and all gadgets are switched off. In the ZC Zone, you are digitally alone.

I looked around at the crowd of others waiting. Who was from where, I like to wonder. I usually go by what people are reading if I can see it, since I think people usually read in their native language regardless of how many languages they can speak or muddle through. There were surprisingly many print books and newspapers—Italian, German, English, Russian and numerous various Asian languages, of course.

Departure time was approaching and the preparations were a model of aplomb. Korean Airlines could launch a spaceship with their efficiency. In their spacious, well-lit gate area with plenty of staff at the ready, a digital clock counting down in full view and a straight arrow disposition to punctuality, the boarding of a KAL plane acquires the buzz of a curtain going up.

We all waited obediently until called and then, when it was at last time to board, the audio system rang out with the Brandenburg Concertos, Bach the boarding meister. Perhaps KAL is the last airline flying to call upon Bach and the like for boarding music, but then again maybe the Brandenburgs are old enough to come back and be taken for new.

Chapter 14

How Much is Involved

I was flying to Korea on the day the President of the United States appeared on TV and told the world he had been surprised how massive the job of President is and "how much it involves."

In my taxi, an elevator version of *Love Me Tender* played in the car. This driver too could not understand me when I asked him to override his auto-lock, and I gave up, again trusting to fate. I wondered if all uncertainties will one day be algorithmically eliminated.

I was whizzed up to my room in a hotel that advertised it had the biggest rooms in Seoul, and surely this room qualified, so high in the cloudy sky that only the Han River flowing below was proof we were still on earth.

Here at least the toilets were still on manual, but I had to laugh when I reviewed the welcome package—the hotel was dripping luxury all over but a separate note announced the Wi-Fi was not free. I called downstairs to question that and *woop*, wiped off. Now, Wi-Fi *is* free.

I had arrived in Korea early enough to plan for dinner with an American woman from San Diego I had been speaking to on the plane. She was joining a group here for further Asian travels the next day and we teamed up and decided to also take in a concert I had spotted in the 'What's On in Seoul' listings. The city has a large cultural center and a busy calendar of offerings. And Seoul, though understandably tense and on edge, especially then when domestic political turmoil boiled alongside the constant ominous proximity of a nuclear North, can be beautiful in spring. There are luxuriant gardens overflowing with azaleas of every color, including a vermillion pink.

In contrast, the US Embassy stood like an austere fortress, encircled by spiked stone walls. A lone American flag flew outside, and a phalanx of Korean police buses were parked to block the gate.

At the concert hall box office, at first the earnest sales woman told us the concert was all sold out, but then she, both shocked at our interest and dismayed at our disappointment, offered consolation. "You can ask the piano company," said she, adding, "Come back at 6."

We wandered around the narrow streets behind the concert hall and thought we had found a cute Korean place for dinner only to learn, from our chatty English-speaking Asian neighbor at the next table, that it was a popular Japanese franchise. So, we were probably chomping down like kid barbarians mixing the wrong sauces on the wrong dishes at a Japanese version of KFC Shrimp and Pork. But the price was right and the food scrumptious.

Back at the box office, indeed the 'piano company' fellow was there and he happily sold us tickets, dead center, third row, $20 each. It seemed he had held on to his VIP or comp tickets too long, and was only too glad to get rid of some. We were seated in the middle of three empty rows, but not an empty seat behind us.

The rest of the audience looked entirely Asian—we were the only foreigners, and sitting conspicuously upfront. There were two glistening Steinways up on the stage.

The fellow who had sold us the seats had also mentioned that the acoustics in the house were so fine that any extra movement we made could bother the performers so, "Don't move too much please," said he. "You can even hear a pin drop and that would disturb the performance," he warned.

But this audience was silent, rapt and devoted and musical magic took hold. One piece was a piano duet by Shostakovich with mesmerizing soft themes I allowed myself to remind me of the Greek composer, Hazidakis. How crazy, to think then of Greece, a place I love, and what it had given up to enter the EU, including the 2000-year-old drachma, then to stay in the EU that was perhaps now en route to disintegration; and did all this back-and-forth and uncertainty justify destroying one of the most ancient currencies in the world?

But then my mind snapped back. Greece, Shostakovich, Korea—time and continents fuse together in a second.

The two women pianists, both professors of music, played fluidly, but they did not smile at all after each piece but only allowed themselves to crack their lips open into something between a grin and a grimace, even at rising applause. Only at the end of the whole concert did they let themselves beam. The audience, perhaps many of their students, crowded around the pianos and we headed back to our hotels.

Outside, the hurly-burly of the early evening street took over where no piano, and surely no pin, could ever be heard.

My talk in Seoul the next day was again rich with thoughtful questions and discussion, but this would be the last one for now.

The next day, I'd be reversing the wheel again.

The *Korean Times* told me that 80% of Korean smartphone users report addiction and addictive behavior and in the *Wall Street Journal* I read that Jack Ma, founder of Alibaba, was predicting more pain than happiness in the next 30 years. Another piece described the likelihood that even though smartcars would be smart, they would not be smart enough to ever avoid accidents entirely.

Wow. Jack Ma, pain merchant, and dumb smartcars.

Oh well, I thought, one of the best things about travel is that it gives you the illusion that you can leave the news that you read behind where you read it.

Chapter 15

Mind the Gap

I was spending one night in Hong Kong again to wind down, see some friends and get ready for that now familiar but still off-balancing transition back home to where, despite my illusions, the news of the day would be waiting for real. President Trump had just recently compounded his admission that the job was tough with an announcement that he had invited the dictator of the Philippines, Duterte, to visit him at the Oval Office—a gesture most President reserve only for persons worthy of admiration—leaving his aides to scramble to explain why a murderous despot was receiving red carpet treatment.

This trip I'd seen against the inescapable scrim of Trump, whose election has elicited non-stop shock and derision from anyone I had met, including my usual Thai taxi driver who, while we had been rolling my bags up the conveyor belt escalator, huffing and puffing, managed still to breath out, "And how about Trump? Could you vote for him?" Meaning "did you vote for him, I hope not." And the next taxi driver I had met later that day said, "Trump? You are American. Why so crazy guy?"

More explaining, more apologizing. I had taken on the Trump obsession just as much as the media, and feeding us obsession seems a conscious Trump tactic, not to mention a Trump craving. Trump eagerly crossed the line between business and entertainment, riding the wave of genre blur. And it is barely a toe-step leap from reality TV to the Presidency of Donald Trump.

Except the stakes are so dreadfully high.

Usually, travel is supposed to detach you from the day-to-day, but once Trump was elected, as an American, I seemed to be wearing him like clothing. His election had attached to me and I could not get free of it. I had become part of the Trump obsession too, if from a distance, as if the politics of my country had become a passion play. Art was following life, life following art, and I was following both.

In the phase between coming and going, doing basic traveler errands can be a useful transition tool and so since I needed a new travel vest, buying it in Hong Kong seemed like an errand that would link present and future, and while the outdoor markets were yet to open, I knew I could find a vest at a camera shop so I set out early for a shop I had located online.

I reached downtown without a hitch on the rapid-fire Hong Kong subway, but when I got to the address, I could see no photo shop upstairs or down.

By then, the light morning rain had become a deluge, and I was trapped in the crumbling door jamb where I thought the photo shop would have been. I waited awhile but the rain did not let up.

I stepped inside a nearby lobby and showed the concierge, a woman, the address I had. She scrutinized the paper, and then grabbed her umbrella and stepped outside, signaling me to join her beneath it as we continued the search. We walked up and down the street, but found no camera shop. Smart phone cameras had probably knocked it out of business. I felt guilty for her taking the trouble, but she seemed to herself be caught up in why a perfectly accurate address did not yield a result. I gave up for a time. But not long.

I had my I-Pad with me, and thought I'd search for some other photo shops in the area but, of course, I needed Wi-Fi. The Landmark Mandarin called out to me, just nearby, a genial and handy Wi-Fi spot. And I was not at all alone.

Nordic Sky was somewhere nearby, as was AirStash018300. And also Hidden Network. I looked around for someone ominous—no one fit the bill.

But my little respite to continue my photo shop search over light breakfast did turn into intrigue for a time.

I could not help overhearing at the next table the birth of a romance, or a business deal, or probably both as a 30-something blond Frenchman who had constantly been checking his phone stood up to greet his appointment who had at last arrived, an exceedingly thin and beautiful Asian woman who sat down and lost no time tossing him questions about his vineyard.

It seemed this was a joint venture in the exploration stage—the woman apparently a potential investor seeking French wine properties and the man apparently in possession of one and in need of a capital infusion. Their discussion moved along to the point where they agreed to another meeting soon where they would bring in other principals to discuss next steps. All in less than 20 minutes, the pace of breaking the ice for business in Hong Kong. He paid, they left, I stayed.

I located another camera shop and took the subway there in about five minutes and did find a handsome vest, all to the good since the outdoor markets never did open that day because of the pounding rain. I drank plenty of tea all day long, slipping in and out of hotels for meetings, more itinerant Wi-Fi, or toilet freeloading, but it all worked well to help me take my leave of Asia.

That night, I went to hear the luscious Hong Kong Philharmonic and took the ferry back to where I was staying with friends. Hong Kong may recede in the mind, but Victoria Harbour never, its light patterns slithering up and down sleek buildings like rippling snake skin. Illuminations such as this do waste energy, but they also inspire, and the trick ahead for all of us is to know the difference.

I drifted back to the news of the world.

Trump and the Republican majority in the US Congress were fixated on repealing the Affordable Health Care Act, Barack Obama's signature domestic policy achievement and the closest the US has ever gotten to a universal health care system, and President Trump had also announced he had just put his son-in-law, who had zero political or diplomatic experience anywhere in the world let alone the Middle East, in charge of rekindling the peace process between Israel and Palestine.

I started to write up some notes from the day's meeting and inadvertently began to use the word 'trumps' as a verb, as I had always done, but I crossed it out. I did not want to use that word anymore because of what it has come to stand for—and could it be an accident that Trump became the family name from Drumpf? Surely Trump's father changed it knowing that for ever more his brand would be a verb tucked into anybody's sentence, and his name would become one and the same with the notion of being one up, taking the advantage, but also 'trumper', 'trompeur', 'trickery, 'trickster'.

"Mind the gap between the platform and the handrail," said the ferry master as we headed down the ramp ready to step aboard.

Indeed, I thought, in the age of Donald Trump, mind the gap between the platform and the rest of your life.

Chapter 16

Begin the Summer on an Island

I connected back to Finland through Bangkok again. The flight is only eight hours, a day flight barely longer than New York to London and it might as well be a sightseeing trip if the weather is clear. But, again, I did not have a window seat, so I planned to read a book or pick a movie, and headed to the restroom to freshen up.

Below, though, through the bathroom window, a blue expanse sparkled. I stepped outside and asked the stewardess what we were flying over and she had to ask the pilot.

Landmarks passing below seem of less and less interest to those who are flying over them, but how can flying over all of Asia become as ordinary as taking a bus?

This time, I skipped the digital map and stayed with real-world sightseeing.

I glued my eyes below through the small window of the plane door. It turned out we were over the Aral Sea with its dried salty lips, ribs of brown dust and no roads, no clouds between me and ground, earth and water painting themselves together. But who remembers the canvas later?

Then the sea was gone. I could make out thin roads like scratches, like the mysterious Nazca plateau in Peru. I could feel the dust and heat on this perfect cloudless day, many worlds at once, and then more roads, more signs of life, like cracks coming into glass over Moscow.

I had been watching a movie about a woman who wonders who she is, and the man who has loved her most of his life and keeps reading their story to her from his diary. So was my lover, the earth, reading to me from below.

I kept looking through the airplane door window or the bathroom window as soon as the 'vacant' sign appeared. The stewardesses did not seem to mind. It was too gorgeous a flight.

An hour from landing or less, the lakes of Finland came into view, lakes as lattice work, and then the brush of touchdown.

We had just swallowed the world in a light gulp of daylight never ending, never clouded and never meeting night.

I usually like to end the summer on an island but this time I was beginning on one, many islands in fact, the Aland Islands. The local bank, Alandsbankenen, or Bank of Aland, is a champion of protecting the Baltic Sea and devotes a large chunk of its profits to its environmental foundation.

But the main innovation is the Bank's credit card and its accompanying Aland Index, which translates the user's purchases into environmental impact automatically, not only in terms of kilos of material used to make or ship the item purchased, but also the cost to the atmosphere of greenhouse gas pollution derived from any burning of fossil fuels used to make or ship the product. The Aland Index, unique and based on methods developed with the accounting firm, KPMG, is pegged to formulas that calculate and integrate the financial costs of environmental degradation, so each Alandsbanken credit card user sees two tallies on the bill. The first tally is the visible familiar retail price of the product—the bill actually due to the bank. The second tally includes the invisible environmental cost, and what would be due to the earth, if the earth were a bank that had a way to charge users for its services. So, for example, polluting the atmosphere has been pretty much free to individual consumers, but the Alandsbanken card applies a price per ton of pollution and notes what that cost would add to the sticker price of the item bought. A cardholder may have charged $100 worth of goods, but the environmental costs might be double that. The customer is thus edified, but has no obligation to pay these environmental costs other than, perhaps, to make a voluntary donation to an environmental cause.

And so the Alandsbanken launched the environmental pricing credit card to educate its consumers on the environmental cost of their spending habits on the theory that this public awareness will over time trigger more thoughtful environmental stewardship policies overall.

Of course, it's a risky business proposition because a side-effect could be to drown the shopper in guilt to the point of not using the card at all, cutting into the card fees and revenue, and the final effect of the Bank's consumer education could be a defunct card and loss of customers.

But Alandsbanken was ready to take that risk because its owners and Board believe that, ultimately, consumers do have to change their spending habits if environmental protection is to be taken seriously—to calculate environmental costs—and Alandsbanken hit the market with the truly first environmental costs credit card in 2016 with no loss at all to business. On the contrary, business has grown.

Spearheaded by Anne-Maria Salonius, head of the Finnish division of Alands Bank, and the Swedish environmental and creative innovator, Mathias Wikstrom, the card is a vanguard product in a world so short on constructive courage. I wanted to see its birthplace, for I too had to contend with my environmental costs—all this travel, flying miles, burning gas. Did my talks to stimulate more environmental investment offset all the miles I fly? Was my so-called 'good' neutralizing my 'bad'?

This is a philosophical and scientific question at its heart, just like the question of when and where to draw the line and act, when and where to resist the served-up patterns, when to refuse to go along, to dare to shake the tree, like Mandela, the whole soul of this trip.

I headed to the Alands, where I would soon see that all land might as well be all water.

It was Friday night, and I flew out from Helsinki and very soon countless islands gleamed below, flung and spun, stones alone in the sea, their mark in the water like the silvery backs of diving dolphins.

Our plane was small and not a jet, and I kept my eye on the props, rotating so fast and reassuringly they disappeared. We seemed to float.

The plan had landed late, but there was no way to rush arrivals. The Alands airport is a one-room terminal, and only the plane is mechanized here. The pilot even helped handle the bags, one by one. My contact from the bank, Tove, picked me up in her Leaf, the electric car made by Nissan. So far, the environment was winning out.

Ten minutes later and ten minutes before my hotel restaurant closed, I was having creamy crayfish soup and listening to the robust chatter of eight Finnish men who'd arrived in the restaurant as late as I had, fishermen or gamblers likely, but in any case a coterie of friends off together for the weekend.

It was 10:20 p.m. but the sun was just about setting and it felt too early to call it a day. I took a walk through the tiny town but all was closed.

The next morning Tove and I were due to take an island overview bike ride. I soon learned that Baltic breakfast time comes in with the sun, so much sun that even at 5 a.m. the blinds have to stay drawn closed or you have to squint just to get dressed.

Block the sun, crave the sun—another extreme swing situation suited to that day in a world of swings. The French were still careening between two candidates in their Presidential election, the creepy Marine Le Pen, who led the right wing National Front Party, and the generous-eyed political newcomer, Emmanuel Macron, who had started a new political party from scratch. Donald Trump had weighed in with a tweet leaning to Le Pen—he had surely begun tweeting more than the birds.

Where is our Macron, I thought. Where is our bright new face to break up the clouds of venom? If Trump was our Le Pen, then where indeed is our Macron?

On the positive side, I saw on BBC One that 82 Nigerian girls who had been kidnapped in 2014 by the terrorist group Boko Haram had been released to their families, but that the President of Nigeria who had secured the release was headed immediately to England for treatment for an undisclosed ailment.

We headed out on our tour. The Alands are a landscape of calm sea, rocks and windy brush, cows allowed to wander in the woods, saunas and boat houses on their own inlets, always land in reference to water. There are some handsome historic buildings, but most recent architecture seemed cheap and drab for the setting, and maybe slapped down into place as if to keep up with the cash flowing into the islands and locked down into a tangible asset apparently, another dichotomy, like a tiny version of China's race to build. But at least if the property investors have an Alandsbanken credit card, they would see the intangible environmental costs of the structures.

The card, though pioneering, does not seem outlandish here. Fairness seems a Finnish virtue. Finland apparently scored so low on the corruption index, the EU had to send inspectors to double-check. Meanwhile, Finnish traffic fines are scaled according to the wealth of the violator. Anders Wiklof, founder of the Alands Bank, once had a fine calculated at $130,000 for speeding on the Aland Islands, being the island group's richest man.

The Alands were not always part of Finland and their history comes down to post boats and pack ice.

The first people had stepped ashore from the east some 6000 years ago but historians have no idea how they survived Baltic ocean gales in open canoes.

The mail route between Sweden and Finland had always crossed the Aland Islands and when the Kingdom of Sweden expanded to include Finland, people needed places to lodge and administrators and clergy had to move across the islands and its numerous inlets, islands, and icy channels. The inhabitants needed a system of communication, ergo mail.

The king set up a mail system based on the distribution of farms. When a farmer received a shipment of mail and moved it on right away regardless of untoward weather, the reward was tax relief. This relay principle depended on healthy sturdy farmers who had to pass a fitness test. A horn signal let the farmer know mail was about to arrive and the farmer, or farmhand, had to be able to run a Swedish mile (10,688 meters) in less than two hours. If not, the farmer lost the mail job. The mail was run this way from Stockholm in Sweden to Turko in Finland once a week, but had doubled its rate by 1757 in a sequence of foot, horse, sleigh, and men on skates pushing chair sledges.

In 1808, though, Sweden lost a war to Russia, and Finland and the Alands were incorporated into the Russian state.

Finally in 1917, the Finns won their independence from Russia and the Alands became part of Finland though enjoying special status still.

A huge four-masted steel barque, the *Pommern*, dates from the early 1900s, and testifies to island power, a once mighty king of the sea but now able only to float with help.

We left the main island for a light lunch in a café on an even smaller island, all buckthorn and berry bush and straight out of smiles of a summer night, me a vagabond in the Baltic under a burning sun.

Here it was so easy to be confused about time when the sun seems never to set. When finally Tove and I split up, it was 5 p.m. but looked like 2.

At the Arkipelag Hotel where I was staying, they fly the flag of the nations of their current guests, and the American flag was snapping. Tove told me that I was the only American at the hotel—she had checked—and so the flag was flying for me. It was the first and likely last flag that would ever be flown in my honor, but in the time of "America First" I could not quite warm to the idea.

I walked down to the sea for a bit. The public dock was draped with a yellow-red caution ribbon because in early May it was still too cold to swim and no diving was allowed even though the depth was shown as nine meters, presumably just enough. I walked on and lost track of the time. I almost missed my dinner with Tove and her family because it seemed to be endless afternoon.

The next and last day in the Alands was Sunday, the day of rest, and here that meant sauna for everyone, even me. Tove and her husband took me to the family sauna house, where outside the birch trees swayed like wands in the wind and the tips of the archipelago were nothing more than arrows of slender rocks.

The sauna was simple, perfectly sealed, a classic wooden house on its own little bay, communally used by friends and family by appointment, with an old map recording all the local names, no longer used, for inlets and land formations nearby.

My hosts heated water in the built-in sauna stove, and used a large copper ladle to toss water on the hot walls to throw off steam.

I stayed in the sauna as long as I could, baking, then stepped outside to cool off with frigid sea water. My skin tingled and burned for a second, but I was exhilarated. High contrast.

Still, the essence of islands is their limits. My Aland indulgences had come to an end. We rinsed off with fresh water we had brought along in thermos bottles and I changed into my city clothes.

Peter Witkof, the Alandsbanken CEO, gave me a lift to the airport, as I began to retrace my steps. He is committed to his bank's green-leaning model, and ready to take the risks that his customers might get sick of his message.

"We must try our best," he said, and no doubt he was, remaking the world of his expertise out of faith and belief, because he could.

As we lifted off the archipelago of puzzle pieces, I spotted wind turbines out at sea turning like toy versions of the propellers again keeping me in the air.

Below, inlets like pockets, uncountable, rock piles and rock tables, flat slabs of stone leading to the sea, recalling the steam of sauna and the sweat rolling down my back, the rinse with hot fresh water heated on the sauna stove, cooled with seawater, a truly Finnish ending to Finland and though I wasn't sure I would, I had surely gotten what I came for.

My freedom is my greatest asset so I used it.

Chapter 17

When in the Course of Human Events

Finally, I got home from what I had started nearly a year before on Christmas Eve, taking in thousands of miles and all seasons and, how welcome, to be able to think of the world as my lover and not be disappointed.

For every day, there is not only the love of place, but the love that comes with being able to live first hand, and experience what is precious. The earth itself, of course, first of all. The American astronauts long ago made the point that from space you can see how unique in the cosmos we are, the blue planet, lone in being endowed with forests, rivers, oceans, and exuberant plants, carbon and water—life made possible.

Jet flight, too, reinforces this sense of earthly privilege, if we take the time to glance out, away from the screen, to be so close to the clouds, to that universal oneness seemingly there to touch but, obviously, forever just a dream of touching.

Democracy too can only be approached, Vaclav Havel, the Czech writer and political leader, said in 1990, the same year Nelson Mandela walked out of prison. Havel was addressing a Joint Session of the US Congress as the newly elected President of the Czech Republic after living most of his life as a dissident who had also been in and out of prison for his outspoken stance against Soviet rule in what was then Czechoslovakia.

Havel told the US Congress: '*As long as people are people, democracy in the full sense of the word will always remain an ideal. One may approach democracy as one would a horizon, in ways that may be better or worse, but which can never fully be attained.*

In this sense you, too, are merely approaching democracy. You have thousands of problems of all kinds, as other countries do. But you have one great advantage: you have been approaching democracy for more than two hundred years, and your journey toward that horizon has never been disrupted by a totalitarian system. Czechs and Slovaks, despite humanistic traditions that go back to the first millennium, approached democracy for

134

a mere twenty years, between the two world wars, and now for a mere three and a half months, since the 17th of November of last year. The advantage you have over us is obvious at once.'

In the age of Trump, perhaps we in America have squandered that advantage?

Perhaps that is the worst of the time of Trump, on the road or at home.

The constantly sickening emphasis on the President's ego and his auto-pilot reproach of any outlying view or critique, leaving to languish any possible progress in governance. Trump only *un*-does, as if his very raison d'etre is to take revenge on all that he himself had no hand in crafting, including the US Constitution itself. As he approached the milestone of his first 100 days in office, he even took aim at the basic checks and balances built into the Constitution to keep one branch of government, including the Executive, from overpowering another. As if to ignite the wrath of his supporters against these most basic controls, he blamed Congressional rules for standing in the way of some of his legislative desires, telling Fox News, a media ally, the Congressional system was "archaic" and "really a bad thing for the country". As his term rolled along, President Trump let fly hundreds of tweets, most of which attacked or mocked any and all who criticized him, ranging from mayors to highly regarded senators to his own Cabinet, to the ordinary people of Puerto Rico, flattened by a demonic hurricane, left on their knees without power, drinking water, shelter, food or the empathy of their President. And when neo-Nazis bloodied African-Americans protesting police brutality, murdering one young woman and in addition chanting "Jews will not replace us", Trump tweeted that there were, even among Neo-Nazis, "some good people". His tweet obsession even rose to the absurdity of alleging that President Obama had wire-tapped Trump's office.

And apropos the rule of law, since his Inauguration, Trump had insinuated he would either dismantle or torpedo numerous laws of the land and hard-won agreements including the Affordable Health Care Act, the Clean Power Plan, the international Paris agreement on climate change, NAFTA and the nuclear power agreement with Iran, negotiated by the Obama Administration with European allies. And, in a boldly defiant act, he fired the head of the FBI, James Comey, who had been looking into charges that some of Trump's advisors may have colluded with Russian agents or authorities to interfere with the results of the 2016 election.

It seemed to me that the Trump approach to governing was dragging democracy slowly out from under our feet like a carpet at a magic show.

But even as the Congress appointed Robert S. Mueller as special counsel to take over the investigation of possible Trump connections to Russian election meddling and Trump's first term rolled on, I began to fret already about a second. Like a bowling ball headed down the alley, Trump seemed to be knocking down Republic and Democratic pins right and left. What if Trump decided to run again on a third party ticket, I wondered, the 'Trump Party', throwing the electoral system into full-fledged electoral chaos? Overturning standards seems to be well within his basic ambitions.

We had already seen in 2000, that the US Supreme Court will not shrink from intervention—the Court stopped a recount in Florida that year that meant, de facto, that the Democrat Al Gore, who had won the national popular vote, had to concede that closely contested state and thereby his win of the electoral college to the Republican George Bush, making Bush President. Rather than throw the whole Presidential electoral system into turmoil, Gore gracefully bowed out. Trump has no such grace. On the contrary, Trump seems to live by chaos.

Third party bids in the US have never truly ignited and seem unlikely to win, but what if Trump's objective would not be to win, necessarily, but put a stick in the eye of his critics, once and for all? Or to drain votes away from both parties as revenge for their abandonment or critique of him?

In the age of Trump, are courts to become more and more the arbiter, rather than the people?

It took about 100 days for the Constitutional Convention to draw up the US Constitution in 1787, but decades of defending it at titanic cost in life, blood and treasure at home and abroad.

It seems inconceivable that we should have to go along quietly while the age of Trump tramples on the very civic foundations that give the Constitution its force, flexibility and strength.

My journey had played fast and loose with time zones and lounges as I ice-skated along on the surface of each day, dabbling in silly luxuries, all transient. And yet, on the road, I could see even more clearly that resistance to mediocrity and rebuilding of the idea of common good is urgent.

I didn't leave my country, it left me, slipping into trends that present violence and blood as if plate decorations and a preoccupation with self—from self-help to please only thyself.

Leadership, like democracy, is ineffable and elusive, but we know it when we see it. In France Emmanuel Macron had won, taking France by storm, upending decades of predictable French party policies in the name of change and fresh approaches, not to mention the rejection of the neo-fascism that the National Front and Le Pen had put forth. But no sooner had his Republic en Marche party won a staggering majority in the National Assembly that pundits on both left and right warned he had too much power even before he had wielded a fraction of it.

Macron defied convention, as did the election of Leo Varadkar to be Prime Minister in Ireland, who seemed to upend every Irish taboo. He was a Hindu elected in Roman Catholic Ireland, and openly gay to boot, in a nation that for decades excluded gay people from Catholic ritual in the most demeaning manner. Many thought such an outsider would have, therefore, left-leaning politics, but turns out he was a right-leaning economics thinker.

Right-leaning, left-leaning, both leading where?

Karl Rove, architect of the second Bush Presidency, told the *New Yorker* magazine in 2003 where he thought America's politics were headed: "I think we're at a point where the two major parties have sort of exhausted their governing agendas."

He was dead right and the Trump election was the result.

Shortly after my return home, news was announced that the U.S. had shot down a Syrian military plane and that this had caused the Russians, a Syrian ally, to discontinue participation in the Hotline—which only the Head of the US Joint Chiefs of Staff, not the individual service chiefs, had permission to use in any case. No Hotline means no failsafe to head off the calamity of an unwanted confrontation. In addition, the Russians said they would consider any plane found flying west of the Euphrates River to be a target, a threat worrying enough for Australia, a staunch US ally, to pull out of the joint air maneuvers, and leaving US planes subject to being shot down just like U.S. airman spy, Gary Powers, in 1960, the only time, at the height of the Cold War, a US plane had been shot down by Russians.

Trump escalating tensions with Russia over Syria fueled by bluster, at the same time as a special prosecutor was looking into potential ties between Trump's campaign and likely Trump himself with Russian manipulation of U.S. election processes. A coincidence? Get tough with Russia while investigators dig around for Russian ties?

I would like to think that American military leaders would not execute an order they deemed to be insane or issued in a fit of Trumpian Presidential pique. Of course, such countervailing of an order given by the US Commander in Chief would be an act of martial law, unprecedented in our nation, but four years and certainly eight could push us to the brink of that.

But failing such a catastrophe, we do have groundwork for how to cope. We are still permitted to enter the US Congress at will pretty much, assuming we can pass through security. It can be inspiring to walk up and down the corridors of the Congress, going from one office to the next, providing a flesh-and-blood conscience and proof that we, the people, do exist.

I had heard that during the Vietnam War, soldiers of the Viet Cong kept live pigs along as they marched through the jungle, drugging the pigs just enough to be quiet if U.S. troops were near, keeping the animals barely alive until the day came to slaughter them for food.

Were we, the American populace, as vulnerable as those pigs, drugged just enough to think all is well, to keep us from making too much noise? When did it happen? Why and when did we stop looking? When did we buy into the story that democracy was like the subway—all you need to do is board and it will take you where you want to go, no maintenance or upkeep required.

And, the trends were getting worse. Take the idea of making a call to express an opinion to an elected official in Washington D.C., still an effective tool despite the overwhelming force of social media.

Wanting to express my opinion that the President should stop insulting London's Muslim Mayor, Sadiq Khan, after the attack on London Bridge in 2017, I called my newly elected Republican Congressman. I got referred to an intern who gave her name as Holly2[0 who while radiating a calm and cool under pressure, plus perhaps hours of phone skills training, politely but robotically took down my comments. I asked her to pass along my wish that the Congressman ask the President to stop his insults of Sadiq Khan, and then to send me a note in writing to let me know what reaction he had gotten from the Trump coterie.

I got a form letter response.

That same week, I called the office of Lamar Alexander, a Republican Senator from Tennessee, to try to learn more about which senators were working on the Senate version of a health care bill. The media had reported a group of 13 senators were working in secret, dead set on replacing the Affordable Health Care Act.

On the same day I had tried to reach Senator Alexander's office, I'd also heard a radio interview with a woman in his home state of Tennessee who was in her 20s whose family had never been able to afford dentistry so she now had no lower teeth. She and her boyfriend had waited hours in line to access a free mobile dental clinic because, said she, referring to the pending Senate rewrite legislation, "… none of these ideas work for me. I am not working either because even though I just got a license to sell insurance, who is going to want to buy insurance from someone with no teeth?"

I had decided to focus on Alexander also because he was a relative moderate and I had some dealings with his office over the years on climate change, a cause to which he had been somewhat sympathetic.

Alexander's office phone rang and rang, then was busy. Then, when I got my turn, a young man with the same pleasant, if orchestrated, phone manner as Holly heard out my questions. First, of my request to know the names of the secret 13 Senators, he said, "let me see if I can get you that list," and put me on hold. But when he returned to the line, he merely said, "all 50 senators have seen the bill … we cannot run down that media story about only 13."

I pressed again but he said, "Ma'am, all I can do is take down your concerns and pass them along so if you could focus on those please in simple terms."

I boiled it down.

Click. Social media, of course, are all there too to communicate with elected officials, and it would have been much easier to send an email or post a like or dislike into the ether. But on the other hand, on the same day, the financial media announced that a new virtual currency named Ether to join the Bitcoin scene, and so it seemed to me the ether was already crowded enough. In an age of crypto-currencies, crypto-politics needed no extra fuel.

While I had been away, the mother of a dear friend had died at age 94, gracefully spitting moral fire until the end. She had been daughter of straight-laced Christian missionaries who nevertheless spent much of her life in some form of resistance to the status quo. Almost to her dying day, when her heart finally stopped, she had stood in the front of the post office in Cooperstown, New York every week holding a protest sign of some sort, mostly to denounce the war instigated by the US in Iraq and Afghanistan.

Cooperstown, of course, is home to the National Baseball Hall of Fame, hallowed ground to baseball fans around the world, symbolic and revered. Set on lovely Otsego Lake, far from any major city, a village of only roughly 1800 residents year round, it is neither rigidly liberal nor conservative, flip-flopping back and forth each cycle. In 2016, Donald Trump did carry Otsego County, which Cooperstown and its tourism dollars dominate, sad to say, but in 2008 and 2012, the County went for Obama.

Of the permanent residents, many are self-employed carpenters, builders, electricians, plumbers, restauranteurs, pest-removers and trash-haulers, as entrepreneurial in their daily business survival as the sprinkling of white collar consultants who also hang out shingles to call in business among the limited number of year-round customers—nearly all but one or two jobs away from financial stress, if not outright insolvency.

In summer, baseball tourists flock into Cooperstown, and they walk up and down Main Street looking for all manner of baseball paraphernalia in what the public relations firm hired to promote Cooperstown has called 'America's Perfect Village'. But nothing is perfect, and in the age of Trump, the per capita income in the area was under $20,000 with wages stagnant, new jobs few, and visits to the Food Pantry climbing.

At the memorial for Nancy, my friend's mother, another stalwart of the protest line at the post office, told the group that one of Nancy's most firm principles of opposition was that the sign she held had to be legible to people driving by the post office who might glance over. Nancy was not interested only in foot traffic.

A gear clicked for me. I live in Cooperstown, and the next day I went to the local general store and bought a bright yellow stiff foam board, way too much sky blue poster paint, and several brushes. I laid the enterprise out on a table in my garden and began forming my letters. My kindergarten lessons in primary colors ought to have prepared me for the result—my blue writing came out a beautiful blue-yellow swirl of green. I smiled and kept going. 'BEWARE OF OUR LOOSE CANNON PRESIDENT' I painted. That should be legible to all, I thought, and clear. 'Loose cannon' seemed concise enough, I thought, in poster terms, though I hesitated as to whether to use the word 'our' as compared to 'the'. I decided I had to associate with the President too, if I believed in the system that had put him there, the whole point of dissenting. The sign would be legible from car or sidewalk. It was my first day as a protestor in the time of Trump.

I joined the regular group at the post office, which is directly across the street from the Hall of Fame, my bright yellow sign indeed eye-catching as some drivers turned their heads though, I admit, they could have simply been just scanning for a parking space.

What was for sure real were the baseball tourists who waved at us as they waited to go into the Hall or when they came out, or took our photos. Also real were the passersby who gave us thumbs up as they walked, and the eleven boys who crossed the street and came over to talk, a junior baseball team from Long Island who asked why we were protesting and took photos with us. And the rugged policeman from Boston who poured out his reservations about Trump for the twenty minutes he joined our line, picking up one of our unused signs from the pile on the lawn, in between rattling off recent stats on the Boston Red Sox, his team, as compared to the New York Yankees, mine, and why for sure the Red Sox were going to win. Politics of the street in Cooperstown also tends to take on a baseball tinge. Only one passerby eyed me and my 'Loose Cannon' sign with disdain and, nearly spitting, declared: "I think he is doing a fantastic job."

Hardly a poll to bet on, but I was aglow. I had acted. But surely a period of ongoing onslaught on institutions by the very President who is sworn to protect those institutions could require moving beyond comfortable protest and opining to more obtrusive tactics.

We can only approach democracy, Havel advised, and so perhaps we will have to re-learn it, like learning to walk again, posture erect. Standing up is what made us different to monkeys, after all.

But America has been slouching instead, a bit lazy when it comes to democratic institutions and civics, and so have I been, taking for granted all that has been given to me, even as I've done my best to improve the world I inherited, sentimentally perhaps.

On the first 4th of July with Trump as President in 2017, a friend convened a few of us to spend the day hand-copying the Declaration of Independence, America's second most venerable document after the Constitution. Written by Thomas Jefferson on behalf of the American colonists to justify the American Revolution against the British Crown and colonial rule, the Declaration was proclaimed on July 4, 1776.

I thought re-copying was surely an excellent way to re-read the document in all its nuanced glory, with me again especially enjoying the fact that

Jefferson and I were born on the same day. With the exception of one vicious paragraph directed at Native Americans that I confess I had never read before, I wrote out every line of the Declaration on the back of several pages of an expired calendar of classic travel posters I had saved.

The calendar, with its parchment-textured paper and stiff cardboard spiral, made the perfect hard lap writing surface. Using a fountain pen, I took one hour and 40 minutes to copy what it had taken Jefferson 17 days to compose. And for all the flaws and failures of the U.S. system of government, the Declaration of Independence remains, to me, a document of all-encompassing eloquence.

It begins: '*When in the course of human events it becomes necessary for one people to dissolve the political bands which have connected them with another and to assume among the powers of the earth, the separate and equal station to which the Laws of Nature and of Nature's God entitle them, a decent respect to the opinions of mankind requires that they should declare the causes which impel them to the separation.*'

In fact, on one of my long Asia flights, I had begun to compose a Declaration of Re-call, aimed at separation from President Trump, outlining his failings and flagrancies. Copying out the original Declaration only refueled this Re-call idea, even if I knew it would likely come to nothing.

In the Declaration, Jefferson laid out the charges the colonists had against King George which, as Jefferson wrote, entitled them to dissolve 'the political bands' that had connected the colonies to the king and Great Britain, noting that, on the other hand, Governments 'long established' should not be changed for 'light and transient causes'.

'*Let facts be submitted to a candid world*,' Jefferson wrote, as he began his enumeration. The charges against King George ranged from ravaging and pillaging the coasts, to taxation without representation and myriad other grievances, all spelled out.

And so what of the list of grievances against Donald Trump in just his first year in office, likely to compound? Humbly, borrowing from Jefferson:

'*He, President Trump, has refused his "Assent to Laws, the most wholesome and necessary for the public good",*

By interfering with ongoing legal actions, such as through the summary firing of the head of the FBI, who was in a position to uncover facts that might have illuminated illegal actions taken or permitted by the President;

He has likely obstructed the Administration of Justice by the above and, in addition,

He has committed what could arguably be called modern day treason, while being in the office of President, in the form of thanking the head of state of our arch-enemy, Russia, for throwing our own US diplomats out of his country; while, while being a candidate for President, he had encouraged that same arch-enemy head of state to spy on his former opponent in the Presidential election;

He has interfered with the free press, prohibited by the Amendment I of the Constitution, by proclaiming publicly and repeatedly that the media, the vehicle of the free press, do not love their country and are an enemy of the people, as retribution for his feeling that the press commented negatively about him.

He threatened to close down the government of the US if the Congress did not vote funds to support a wall between the US and Mexico, an explicit undermining of his oath since protecting the US Constitution means to protect the United States government.

He exploited his Presidential pardon power by pardoning a criminal who had subverted national laws and on whom justice has been served, where the verdict had not been dubious, and did not allow five years to pass before considering the case.

He lied to the public that he had no business dealings with Russia, the above referenced arch-enemy nation, even as documents have revealed he had been entertaining the possibility of building a tower bearing his name in Moscow and though his own son and other business associates had had meetings with Russian counterparts during the election, where the election was discussed.

He has egregiously put the Republic and the world at risk of nuclear war by taunting and threatening foreign governments able to conduct such nuclear war, including at the United Nations where, without prior authority from the Congress, he declared that the United States would have no choice but to totally destroy another nation, namely North Korea, a blatant and unprecedented abuse of power that, in any case, could not be undertaken without an Act of War declared by Congress.

And, in a flagrant, public and illegal attack on the people's rights to free speech as protected unequivocally and without reservation in Amendment I of the US Constitution, he has explicitly called for punishment of protestors who chose to avail themselves of this right by kneeling during the US national anthem as an act of objection to racial injustice, stating that such protestors should be fired from their lawful positions, thereby violating outright and undeniably the President's Oath of Office to preserve, protect and defend the Constitution and, as such, an impeachable offense.

We, therefore, the citizens of the United States, do Re-call this President, and for the support of this Declaration, we mutually pledge to each other our lives, our Fortune and our Sacred Honor.'

Travel braids reality and absurdity, bubbles the mind, takes dreams to heights and down again. Re-call of a US President is unprecedented.

A year after my odyssey had begun, and as Trump's first year in office was coming to an end, the misanthropic President of the United States spent his Christmas Eve shooting ego-maniacal tweets into the most holy religious evening raining suspicion on FBI officials he continued to accuse of chronic bias against him. And barely had 2018 kicked off, than Trump called legislative leaders to the White House to discuss immigration legislation, only to denigrate Haiti and African nations as "shithole" countries, earning the admiration of the Daily Stormer, a neo-Nazi website, which commented: "this is encouraging and refreshing, as it indicates Trump is more or less on the same page as us with regards to race and immigration." The President of the United States was embraced by neo-Nazi thinking, and most of the Congress took that in its stride.

As 2018 rolled along, so did the volatile President of the United States, careening between headlines, one day announcing a high stakes summit with the erratic President of North Korea, and the next, parrying allegations that he had an affair with a porn star named Stormy Daniels, had hush money paid to her, and then lied about it. Unchecked and unbowed, he unilaterally moved the US Embassy in Israel to embattled Jerusalem, tossing out years of careful diplomacy and triggering a new wave of horrific violence and, just as unilaterally, pulled the U.S. out of the hard won international agreement to limit Iran's nuclear arsenal, spurning entreaties to remain from long-standing US allies. Taking executive branch prerogatives to a grotesque extreme, Trump treated the US Presidency as if it were his own personal toy chest.

Benjamin Franklin was right to wonder if we in the US could keep the new Republic the Constitution had created. But we must. For that, to strive constantly to protect the ideal, is the only way to resist the demeaning and dangerous age of Trump. With what effort and how—that will be for each of us to say.

'Get out of Jail Free' cards exist only in the game of Monopoly. But Americans may need to keep some handy to win over the guards. Resisting trickery will have gotten us into jail; and so it might have to be trickery that gets us out.

Epilogue: Banging and Whimpering

Not with a bang but a whimper. So wrote the poet, T.S. Eliot, on how the world would end. I had to wonder which way we'd go myself, as 2019 dawned.

The new year found me in Latin America, yet another continent far from home but not from the political science of the road. In Buenos Aires, the city was closed up tight for the long Christmas holiday period, except for the milongas, outdoor tango soirees, where the people of the city come together to dance the night away. The tango might as well be lifeblood in Argentina--with its mournful sexiness and couples held tight. The dance was once banned outright as seditious and sinful by religious conservatives, then for being too radical and working class by anti-union governments, then nearly wholly lost for a while to the culture until the youth of the upper social echelons discovered it, took it to Europe where it became chic, and then brought it home, rehabilitated. Now the tango is everyone's again, and milongas simmer with human desire laced into the collective memory of the nation's political ebb and flow.

Just outside my hotel, in the small buzzing plaza, the restaurants and cafes cleared an area for dancing, and waiters strung tiny lights among the pine and palm trees to turn nightfall back into a lasting dusk. A master tango dancer who called himself "El Indio" was the host of this milonga, and he carefully set up his retro music speakers, stringing power cords precariously also up in the trees, encircled by a hundred people or so, watching as intently as they were also waiting their chance. But first, El Indio had to set the mood. He wore a crisp tuxedo and took command with his partner, a lithe woman in a silky black dress flashing with tassels. The two dipped and spun together so smoothly, it was as if their steps were writing the music that played as they danced. Some in the crowd sang along with the familiar playlist; all watched each exotic bend, as if trying to memorize it. Then, El Indio passed the hat, the signal the performance had ended and the moment would soon come for all to take the floor. One by one--women, men, all ages, tattooed and not, gray-haired, pink-haired, gay and straight couples—deposited their knapsacks or purses up around the base of the central palm tree, to cordon off their possessions within the circle of dancing. While they were deep into the tango mood, no thief could snatch a thing without breaking through the scores of couples where all would see. A tango circle became a bank vault.

And then the music never stopped, as the people seemed to lose themselves in the sensuality of the tango steps they knew by heart and the songs they held in common, twirling and locking into each other in a gentle competition between those who knew well the dance, and those who could only try their best.

The people were improvising their low-cost New Year's entertainment, as they had to improvise each day. Inflation still ran rampant in Argentina, cash machines were out of pesos, banks were closed, and the taxi drivers hungered for US dollars anyway because, as one driver told me "the peso cannot buy you anything for long and so we cannot plan how we will live." As he drove me from the airport when I arrived, he had also said that when Americans had elected Donald Trump, "I could not believe my eyes."

January first was a languid lazy morning, but not without its disturbing front page news. Back home, the Democrats were digging in deep against the wall that Donald Trump had promised his followers he'd build on the southern border of the country to keep out the immigrants he derided as all-criminal, all-dangerous, a wall even the US Immigration Service did not think would serve as a useful remedy. But to win out, Trump would eventually circumvent Congressional budget authority by declaring a military emergency at the border in order to tap into the defense budget to build the wall.

At one point, Trump would even gleefully preside over a shutdown of the whole US government, causing nearly half a million Federal employees to work without pay for nearly a month to keep essential services, going, including airport and border security. Trump bragged, "I will be glad to own the shutdown," rather than compromise when the Democrats proposed a budget that did not include all he thought the wall would cost.

Trump had also just flip-flopped on an earlier statement that he planned to withdraw US troops from Syria right away. Now, on New Year's morning, after much criticism from stunned American military commanders who disagreed and with whom he had failed to consult, Trump casually announced he was slowing down the withdrawal, as if waging the pace of war was as routine as pumping a gas pedal.

But not all my angst could be blamed on Trump. Opposition to him was beginning to appear, but a bit haplessly. Elizabeth Warren, a high-profile US Senator, had finally officially declared her long-assumed Presidential candidacy, despite an ill-advised effort to prove she was one of the people, as it were. Warren had announced that she had Native American ancestry, then set out to establish the fact with a genetic test that showed only that she had the thinnest of Native-American bloodlines, triggering derision from some tribal elders. Trump, of course, too weighed in, invoking the name of an iconic Native American princess to ridicule the Senator he now referred to as "Pocahontas" in his tweets.

And in other columns of the front page, little comfort. A headline proclaimed "Wielding Rocks and Knives, Arizonans Attack Self-Driving Cars" a slashing of tires that was one of nearly two dozen attacks in Chandler, home of Waymo, a driverless-car company spun-off from Google, according to the New York Times. People in America were on edge to the point of attacking machinery, just like the Luddites.

And so as Trump passed the mid-point of his first term, civil society seemed to be whimpering toward the dark ages and political discourse too.

By spring 2019, at least 15 Democratic contenders for President had emerged, many women among them, and all already bunched together by Trump who dismissed them "the Democratic far left." And none of the Presidential hopefuls seemed to be capturing the public imagination. They were each in their own way too broadly thematic and calibrated, and all way too early. And all no doubt assuming that Trump would be significantly politically damaged by the long-awaited report by the Special Counsel Robert Mueller--which had been looking for two years into whether there had been collaboration between the Trump campaign and Russian interference in the 2016 Presidential election, as well as Trump's payments to paramours, his borrowing from foreign banks, and possible campaign finance violations. But, when the report came out, au contraire.

Mueller finished his inquiry in March and submitted his report to the US Attorney General, William Barr, as was the specified process, on a Friday afternoon. By the end of the weekend, Barr had made public a letter he had sent to key Members of Congress from both parties, summarizing the Mueller report findings. Barr told the world that Mueller's investigation had found no evidence of conspiracy or collusion with the Russians, even though it was doubtless that various Russians had held meetings with

Trump operatives offering to help Trump's campaign, including by providing "dirt" on Hillary Clinton.

As regards the second prong of the investigation and whether various Trump controversial actions amounted to criminal obstruction of justice, Barr also made public the fact that Mueller had, for whatever reason, punted. Said Barr, "The Special Counsel states that 'while this report does not conclude that the President committed a crime, it also does not exonerate him.'"

So, Barr continued: "The Special Counsel's decision to describe the facts of his obstruction investigation without reaching any legal conclusions leaves it to the Attorney General to determine whether the conduct described in the report constitutes a crime...After reviewing the Special Counsel's final report on these issues...Deputy Attorney General Rod Rosenstein and I have concluded that the evidence developed during the Special Counsel's investigation is not sufficient to establish that the President committed an obstruction-of-justice offense."

No smoking guns, either for part one or two.

Trump himself was effervescent. "A total vindication" he proclaimed from his Florida mansion, where he had spent the weekend when Barr's letter hit the media, ignoring the report's caveat of non-exoneration. And within minutes of hearing the Attorney General's summary, Trump set the tone of reprisal: "There are a lot of people out there that have done some very, very evil things, some bad things, I would say some treasonous things against our country...and hopefully people that have done such harm to our country—we've gone through a period of really bad things happening—those people will certainly be looked at."

Despite the air of vengeance and intimation of treason by the duly serving, many of Trump's supporters were euphoric too and the sum of the mood seemed to be that if indeed Trump himself had done something wrong, it wasn't *that* wrong. Mueller himself had impeccable credentials, and so if Mueller could not find unequivocal proof, the average person had the right to conclude that proof did not exist.

But barely a day had passed before Trump trampled on his own apparent good news. Inexplicably, Trump's Administration resurrected the abandoned political battle over the signature Obama achievement in US public policy, the Affordable Health Care Act. As soon as he had been elected, Trump and the Republican Congress had tried several times unsuccessfully to repeal the law—they had no credible alternative and the law had become the bedrock health insurance program for millions of Americans.

Inexplicably, Trump pushed the Mueller report off the front page by authorizing the Justice Department to seek to negate the health bill once and for all in the courts, again trying to circumvent the Congressional legislative process that had laid the matter to rest. And also inexplicably, Trump took specific aim at the one provision that even Republicans had sought to protect throughout their failed attempts to repeal—the pre-existing conditions proviso. This established that private insurers could not exclude insurance coverage for persons who had pre-existing medical conditions. The Catch-22 had haunted the sick in America until the Affordable Health Care Act--if you were ill or at risk, you could be dropped from your health insurance plan if your bills became too high, or not be able to get insurance at all.

At times, it seems that the news must be full of typos. Surely, I thought, the New York Times must have meant to print that Trump would *not* go after pre-existing conditions. But there was no typo. Trump had indeed authorized his legal team to be sure to also remove the only protection Americans have against losing their health insurance when they need insurance most.

This gave the Democrats a second wind—Trump had put himself squarely against a majority of Americans, for whom the pre-existing conditions clause had become sacred. The Democrats, in fact, had won their majority in the House in November largely by campaigning against Trump's attitudes to health insurance and lost no time taking up the health care mantle again.

Trump's resuscitated battle on health care seemed needlessly aggressive.

But the time of Trump has given us the tone of Trump, a low brow inflammatory style that seems not only derisive but angry, vengeful and scornfully devil-may-care. Trump does not lead, he lashes out.

Meanwhile, extremism in the world seems to compound itself, and one has to wonder is the tone of Trump symptom or cause? The "yellow vest" cadres in Paris emerged in 2019 to protest a rise in gasoline taxes but then turned violent and burned cafes on the Champs Elysees, while the far-right political party Alternative for Germany continued to gain power, even though the German state has renounced any hint of Nazi-like expression for nearly a century. In Hungary, Victor Orban's Fidesz party, or so-called Civic Alliance, continued to whip up the Hungarian people against all foreigners. And in Brazil, Jair Bolsonaro, an ideologue with no political experience whatsoever but plenty of Trump-like rhetoric was elected President on the slogan "Brazil before everything and God above all." Praising the former Brazilian dictatorship and white supremacism, he also proudly declared he would rather let the Amazon jungle burn down than surrender Brazilian sovereignty to those who would protect the rainforest. Bolsonaro took his victory lap to the White House, basking in the praise of Trump.

Meanwhile, President Trump continued to deride and disrupt the traditional democratic alliances of goodwill, such as NATO and the EU, leaving heads spinning as to what the America really stands for.

So, the time of Trump has come to mean, at the minimum, confusion. How is it possible that just after Trump's election, an ordinary taxi driver in Asia was attuned enough to asked me "why so crazy guy?" but two years later, Trump is an entrenched as ever, Republicans only once stepping up in numbers to challenge him. When he declared the national emergency to allow himself to dig into the defense budget for funds for the anti-immigration wall, 12 Republicans crossed the aisle to support a bill blocking his declaration. But still, Trump vetoed the bill and there were not enough votes in the Congress to over-ride him.

Trump, two years in, is on a roll.

Political science has never been truly scientific, but like all other dimensions of the world post WWII, theories of what constitutes political wisdom are being upended and disrupted by instant flow of information, fake or real.

Politic dialogue is now a Cuisinart of commentary, or as a friend said to me, "talk is the new currency."

But meanwhile, long-respected systems disintegrate and the world now seems to tolerate formerly intolerable gray areas.

If Trump is not impeached and has not committed a crime that can be proven, is he fit nevertheless to lead the US and the world? Is his judgement sufficiently balanced, his motivations sufficiently selfless?

The team of scorpions I envisioned as Trump announced his first Cabinet picks just after the 2016 election indeed eventually take shape, called the "Team of Vipers" in a book by a White House insider one year later, who couldn't contain himself from writing an expose about White House dysfunction and the rivalries of self-interest. Sordid trends and conflicts of interest established the day after Trump's election have solidified and remained.

Re-call the President? Re-call indeed. The next chance to Re-call will be the next election in the US.

Protest? Yes. In Buenos Aires, the Mothers of the Plaza de Mayo still protest every week at the central square in full sight of the pastel pink Presidential palace, demanding authorities explain what happened to their missing children nearly forty years ago, when Argentina was in the grip of a dictatorship. In that infamous "dirty war," the nation's democracy died in full sight of the world. The protests of the mothers do not dissipate; the failure of democracy leaves gashes for a long time.

And at home, outside my post office in Cooperstown, every Wednesday, still, the regular protest group assembles. I've made a new sign—"End racism for everyone's sake"--but I am not on the sidewalk often enough.

And if there was no collusion in the Trump-Russia matter, does this mean Trump's innocence? Was there perhaps a wink? Trump the deal maker knows precisely how far to go in words, in writing. And no one in the Trump fold who was approached by the Russians reported the incident to the FBI or any government agency.

Even the denunciation of Trump by his former fixer, Michael Cohen, who himself acted illegally to handle some of Trump's questionable dealings, testifying before a US Congressional committee and warning the nation that Trump is a "racist…conman…cheat" has not stuck. Cohen is going to jail. Trump is not.

So, the time of Trump seems to be transforming the very nature of politics and political science, defining them as one-upping, one down-ing, revenge and risky rhetoric the foundation of decision-making on which thousands of lives may depend. Build a wall? Congress says no. Trump declares a national security emergency to ignore their legitimate power. A flagrant attack on Constitutional checks and balances, but too many members of Congress hold back. Trump gets his way.

The time of Trump is the politics of the petulant, now gradually transcending the man himself.

And in the process, what has statesmanship become? The art of leadership or the art of winning?

Democracy can stand only if there is a common view of what is common sense, and the courage to defend the common interest. Whimpering or banging? In the time of Trump, either way, we lose.

About the author

Paula DiPerna is a writer and frequent media and conference speaker on a variety of subjects, particularly environmental and political issues.

As writer and Vice President for International Affairs for the Cousteau Society, she worked with explorer and film-maker Jacques-Yves Cousteau and co-produced numerous documentary films travelling worldwide on the famous vessel *Calypso*. DiPerna has been widely published internationally in newspapers and magazines, and her book, *Cluster Mystery: Epidemic and the Children of Woburn, Mass.* was the first book to be written about an infamous leukemia cluster possibly associated with contaminated drinking water.

DiPerna has written other non-fiction books, including *Oakhurst: The Birth and Rebirth of America's First Golf Course*. Her novel, *The Discoveries of Mrs Christopher Columbus: His Wife's Version* is a fictional journal that might have been kept by the wife of Columbus.

DiPerna was a candidate for the US Congress in 1992.

Made in the
USA
Middletown, DE